When Love Speaks

Adam O'Riordan was born in Manchester in 1982, and educated at the universities of Oxford and London. In 2008 he was awarded an Eric Gregory Award and was Poet-in-Residence at the Wordsworth Trust in Grasmere. He is the author of *In the Flesh*. He lives in London.

When Love Speaks

Poetry and prose for weddings,
relationships and married life

EDITED AND INTRODUCED BY
Adam O'Riordan

VINTAGE BOOKS
London

Published by Vintage Classics 2011

1 3 5 7 9 10 8 6 4 2

Selection and editorial material © Adam O'Riordan 2011
The Acknowledgements on pages 239–244 constitute an extension
of this copyright page

The moral right of the editor has been asserted

Vintage
Random House, 20 Vauxhall Bridge Road,
London SW1V 2SA

www.vintage-classics.info

Addresses for companies within The Random House Group Limited can be found at:
www.randomhouse.co.uk/offices.htm

The Random House Group Limited Reg. No. 954009

A CIP catalogue record for this book
is available from the British Library

ISBN 9780099541387

The Random House Group Limited supports The Forest Stewardship Council (FSC),
the leading international forest certification organisation. All our titles that are printed
on Greenpeace approved FSC certified paper carry the FSC logo. Our paper procure-
ment policy can be found at www.rbooks.co.uk/environment

Printed and bound in Great Britain by
CPI Bookmarque, Croydon CR0 4TD

This book is for Alice,
with all my love

Contents

The Welcome

The Declarations

The Vows

The Giving of Rings

The Blessing of the Marriage

The Recession

Introduction

A few years ago, standing beside a rose arch on a late-summer afternoon in upstate New York, I found myself suddenly overcome with nerves. My old friends from university, the bride and groom, were seated before me and behind them a sea of expectant faces. My mouth was dry and the microphone felt huge and clumsy in my hand. I was about to read a poem by W.B. Yeats when it struck me not just how much depended on the reading but how arduous the process of choosing the right words for this rite of passage had been.

After hours of poring over anthologies the couple had chosen 'He Wishes for the Cloths of Heaven'. It had seemed the right poem, not just because the bride worked in fashion or the groom first tried to woo her as an exchange student at Oxford by reading Yeats aloud in her room, but also because the high romance of the tone was balanced by the delicate repetitions and the vulnerability of the poet's offering, 'I have spread my dreams under your feet; / Tread softly because you tread on my dreams'.

As I read, I felt the tension dissipate, and with the readings that followed and the exchange of vows, a sense of togetherness spread through the guests, many of whom had been strangers earlier. It felt as if some great glowing net had been cast over us. The poems read seemed to resonate not just with the poetry readers in the audience, a decade out of university there were still a few, but with others too, colleagues from the bride's father's factory, doctors, bankers, lawyers, people who weren't supposed to like poetry.

As I retook my seat I remembered just how many of the books we had looked at that purported to contain wedding poems but were, in fact, full of clichés and tired-sounding greeting-card rhymes. It occurred to me that an anthology of writing to mark and memorialise this act of union would surely be one of the most pleasurable, and necessary, types of book to edit and to read.

So in this spirit I set to work compiling *When Love Speaks*. I wanted to gather together poems and passages that captured some of the strangeness of the wedding day, the tensions, the anticipation, as well as the moments of uncommon happiness. Nobel prize-winner Seamus Heaney's poem 'Wedding Day' is a perfect example, combining myriad elements of the day as experienced by the groom:

> I am afraid.
> Sound has stopped in the day
> And the images reel over
> And over…

the speaker tells us at the poem's opening before asking of his new wife at the poem's close: 'Let me/ Sleep on your breast to the airport'.

From Heaney's contemporary, Michael Longley, we have the poem 'No Continuing City', where the voice of a man on the eve of his wedding dismisses the memories of lovers who have come before; telling his wife-to-be:

> …she is welcome,
> Advising her to make this last,

> To be sure of finding room in me
> (I embody bed and breakfast) –
> To eat and drink me out of house and home.

While Derek Mahon, who together with Heaney and Longley form a golden generation of contemporary Irish poets, imagines in his 'Preface to a Love Poem' that:

> The words are aching in their own pursuit
> To say 'I love you' out of indolence
> As one might speak at sea without forethought

and in doing so introduces that note of pervasive, barely restrained, ecstasy we might recognise from a wedding day.

Celebratory, strange and containing a sense of wonder, these three poems set the tone for the anthology: a selection of prose and poetry in which the reader might wander aimlessly or, with the help of the index, quickly pick out something specific to read aloud, words that might be returned to long after the wedding day had passed.

So where to begin? The poems and passages have been divided into six sections, the title of each taken from a traditional order of service for a wedding: The Welcome, The Declarations, The Vows, The Giving of Rings, The Blessing of the Marriage and The Recession. Though religious in origin, each term has been interpreted as broadly as possible.

The Welcome contains poems and passages celebrating the occasion and setting the tone, from Charles Darwin musing on the pros and cons of marriage, to Robert Louis Stevenson writing on falling in love. Next comes The Declarations, personal expressions of love and togetherness, from the knowing lyrics of Princeton professor and part-time rock musician Paul Muldoon to poet and apothecary John Keats' impassioned writing in his poem 'Bright Star'.

Next are The Vows, more formal expressions of commitment and union, like James Fenton's 'Hinterhof' in which he declares, 'Stay true to me and I'll stay true to you'. The Giving of Rings section is concerned with capturing the wedding day itself, from Charles Dickens' description of a wedding in *The Pickwick Papers* to Edgar Allan Poe glorying in the sound of church bells and the 'world of merriment their melody foretells!'

The next section is The Blessing of the Marriage, which contains wisdom and advice on marriage and married life from voices as varied as the Pre-Raphaelite poet Christina Rossetti to an Edwardian guide on *Modern Marriage and How to Bear It*. The final section, The Recession, looks at marriage over time, probing how love is both tested and endures, as in 'In Our Tenth Year' by Simon Armitage, 'A decade on, now we astound ourselves; / still two, still twinned but doubled now with love'.

Within these sections, the poems are grouped so that one poem or passage might shed light upon the other, echoing similar tones. Scottish poet Kathleen Jamie's poem of everyday intimacy 'Duet', in which the voice declares, 'I am the music of the string duet / In the Métro... Again and again I discover that I love you', sits alongside Irish poet Leanne O'Sullivan's 'Comrades', addressed to 'My heart's saviour, / my best friend'. While Edmund Spenser's 'Amoretti' (1595) and Alice Oswald's 'Wedding' (1996) display a communality of feeling that spans the centuries as well as poets' continuing inventiveness when looking for metaphors and images to describe love and togetherness. For Oswald, love is, among other things, 'a sail' and 'a swallowtail'.

The anthology contains a number of epithalamia ('epithalamium' is a good-looking but disconcertingly formal word meaning, simply, a poem composed for a bride), from sixteenth-century poet and later Dean of St Paul's cathedral, John Donne, to Scottish poet and quizmaster, Roddy Lumsden. Written some five hundred years apart, the epithalamia of Donne and Lumsden stand as testament to the ongoing draw of the occasion to poets. In 'An Epithalamion or Marriage Song on the Lady Elizabeth and Count Palatine being Married on St Valentine's Day', Donne declares:

> Hail Bishop Valentine, whose day this is;
> All the air is thy diocese,
> And all the chirping choristers

In Lumsden's complex and demotic 'On a Promise (an epithalamium)' the voice in the poem describes the act of giving over and letting go that occurs when two people are married:

> And if not caution, then its conduit
> Is given to the wind. A giddy ship
> Of fools and family, rocking loose

Both poems fizz with metaphysical intensity as language is put to work mapping the machinations of the soul.

When Love Speaks contains some poems and passages to be declared aloud in churches and register offices, like the august offerings from Algernon Charles Swinburne and William Morris, and others to be reflected on in private, such as the poem 'My Second Marriage to my First Husband' or the passage from Edith Wharton that reveals love and marriage, commitment and longing, to be possessed of a greater complexity than some of the happier pieces in the anthology might suggest.

Not all of the poems and passages are explicitly about weddings or married life. Some have been chosen to stand for the things we think of when we think of two people beginning a life together. We have the devotional poetry of seventeenth-century Anglican priest George Herbert. Here a man talking to his God might be used, for our purposes, as a vow of devotion exchanged by a couple. In his poem 'A Wreath', which opens the Vows section, Herbert offers a 'wreathed garland of deservèd praise' to 'Thee, who knowest all my ways, / My crooked winding ways, wherein I live'. While the aptly named Reverend Church's version of the story of the Sirens from Homer's *Odyssey* stands as a warning about temptation.

There are words to cement the ceremony but also words that capture and reflect the moments before and after the celebration. Like Thomas Hardy's 'The Dawn After the Dance', where 'a new strange bond between our days was formed' but in which he warns at its close 'the vows of man and maid are frail as filmy gossamere'.

The wisdom gathered in the book is not always the fruit of happy marriages. The meeting of Gertrude Coppard and Walter Morel in the passage from D.H. Lawrence's *Sons and Lovers* portends to darker times ahead. We have Emma in *Madame Bovary* already dreaming of escape and life outside the confines of her marriage:

Sitting on the grass that she dug up with little prods of her sunshade, Emma repeated to herself, 'Good heavens! Why did I marry?'

Neither are all the marriages in the anthology conventional. We hear poet and gardener Vita Sackville-West describe her first meeting in 1920 with her future husband, the diplomat and later Member of Parliament Harold Nicholson. She records him being 'very young and alive and charming'. Theirs would go on to be a famously open relationship, catering for the bisexuality of man and wife, but one at the core of which remained a genuine tenderness. I hope that these poems and passages will be of value to partnerships and pairings of all kinds.

As well as Nobel prize-winners, like Lessing and Heaney, and canonical and popular texts, I wanted to bring to readers poetry from contemporaries whose invention and artistry I love. Clare Pollard, whose poem 'To My Fiancé' opens the book, tells how 'At first, engaged, unused to jewellery, / I turn the ring like a loose tooth', while Frances Leviston in her arresting and assured poem 'Dragonflies' describes observing the mating insects:

> I think of delicate clumsinesses
> lovers who have not yet mentioned
> love aloud enact.

Inspired by the dragonflies coupling in flight and resistance to stasis, Leviston asks finally, 'How can I demand love stop, and speak?'

Paul Batchelor shows that contemporary poetry's use of the mythological need not be dry or inaccessible. In his sensual and visceral 'Pygmalion's Prayer to Venus' the voice in the poem prays to the goddess that she might:

> Grant my idiot wish for flesh & blood
> and that will be enough, more than enough,

> for one who only ever worshipped you,
> your belly: cedar-gold; your shoulder: cedar-sweet

While Jacob Polley in a beautiful and brutal six-line poem, in a tradition come down from De Sade and Baudelaire, muses on a ring made from a dor beetle: 'scavenger on slug flesh, shit eater / I wear you on my wedding finger', demanding, 'At the end of love, start burrowing.'

A similar affecting strangeness is shown in the work of the preceding generation of poets. Fiona Sampson describes the entrapments and snarings between two lovers in 'World Asleep' in the final section, The Recession. She tells how: 'My fingers on your latch / are tender when they lift the tongue'. In the same section Scottish poet and novelist John Burnside in 'Anniversary' captures 'unrecorded love' in 'some blind creature circling the roof'. These wilder imaginings sit alongside the touching tenderness of poems like Andrew Motion's 'A Goodnight Kiss', where he holds his lover's 'amazingly light body' in his arms and Linda Chase's 'Kiss in the Dark', where the object of the poem in growing old has:

> thickened around the middle
> like a successful custard
> on a wooden spoon

And yet, Chase adds, in a note of partial promise and erotic potential at the poem's close:

> She loves you, nevertheless.
> At arm's length, she ventures
> a first caress in the dark.
> Will you go on from there?

So this anthology, while being celebratory, aims to capture as many various moods and moments as exist in any one relationship. The idea of 'spring' and 'growth' and 'planting', recorded in various forms, is a touchstone of the book. Be it in Edward Thomas' poem 'Sowing':

> It was a perfect day
> For sowing; just
> As sweet and dry was the ground
> As tobacco-dust

or the passage from Katherine Swift's *The Morville Hours*, where she describes the passion for one's garden as: 'a love affair… the very smell intoxicates like the smell of a lover.'

But the anthology tries not to rely purely on the poetic. In it you will find the *Stanford Encyclopedia of Philosophy*'s online entry for 'Love' as well as a definition of being 'wed' from a 1926 *Dictionary of Modern English Usage*. In his masterful work *The Lodger: Shakespeare on Silver Street*, Charles Nicholl reveals the bard's involvement in a 'handfasting', a traditional ceremony where 'gifts would often be exchanged in token of the betrothal'. The idea of gift giving is brought to life by Irish poet Eavan Boland in her poem 'The Black Lace Fan My Mother Gave Me'. It speaks of a gift from her father to her mother courting in Paris, where:

> The past is an empty café terrace.
> An airless dusk before thunder.
> A man running

There is comic writing from G.K. Chesterton in 'A Defense of Rash Vows' and from P.G. Wodehouse, who tells us: 'Dudley Pickering was not a self-starter in the motordrome of love'. These appear alongside finds made among books of Victorian and Edwardian etiquette and wedding comportment. In the 1910 *Modern Marriage and How to Bear It* Maud Churton Braby declares, 'I believe one can be fairly happy in marriage without love, once the ardours and madness of extreme youth have passed' but cautions that 'Without respect one can never be anything but wretched'. There is also an Edwardian piece promoting the merits of sport for couples.

There are poems in the anthology that perhaps can't really claim a rightful place: gate-crashers, voices that might speak out when the priest asks if anyone knows of any lawful impediment. Sir Thomas Wyatt's 'Whoso List to Hunt' is a plaintive poem of suppressed passion thought to be written about Henry the VIII's wife Anne Boleyn. Smitten by the unattainable Boleyn, Wyatt compares her to a 'hind', or deer, he may not hunt:

> There is written, her fair neck round about:
> '*Noli me tangere*, for Caesar's I am,
> And wild for to hold, though I seem tame.'

I imagined the poem being picked up and mused on by some anxious best man with an undeclared longstanding love for the bride or offered as some kind of votive to the ghosts of former lovers that may flit across the minds of the betrothed at some point on their wedding day.

The second is W. B. Yeats' 'The Collar-Bone of a Hare'. The poem challenges the reader to find inside this anthology the proof that Yeats' vision of changing 'my loves while dancing / And pay but a kiss for a kiss' is untrue. While Lady Grizel Baillie's eighteenth-century song of longing 'Werena My Heart

Licht I Wad Dee' reminds us every marriage has a hinterland, and lovers left behind.

In compiling an anthology such as this and living with the poems and passages, it is hard not to develop favourites. W.B. Yeats could have filled half the book, so could John Donne. And in the selecting from Shakespeare I have tried to avoid the obvious choices. The book's title comes from Biron's speech in *Love's Labour's Lost*:

> And when Love speaks, the voice of all the gods
> Makes heaven drowsy with the harmony.
> Never durst poet touch a pen to write
> Until his ink were temper'd with Love's sighs

Literature has the power to both capture and invoke the wonder, angst and dizzying happiness of a wedding day. I hope that in this anthology there are pieces that do just that. Some poems and passages stand out for their clarity and their rightness of tone: emotion and intellect perfectly coupled. The words themselves ideally suited to send any pair off together into married life. None more so than Sir Philip Sidney's 'The Bargain', which reads like an elegantly simple solution to the complex puzzle that love can sometimes be. It therefore seems right to give him the last word:

> My true love hath my heart, and I have his,
> By just exchange one for another given:
> I hold his dear, and mine he cannot miss,
> There never was a better bargain driven.

Adam O'Riordan, 2011

The Welcome

CLARE POLLARD

For My Fiancé

At first, engaged, unused to jewellery,
I turn the ring like a loose tooth –
lying in bed aware of its touch, like the touch
of a finger to thigh. Eyes open to the silvered blinds,
I imagine outside: how the lakes will spangle
and bloat, skies clear and then pummel with storms, rivers
break banks, how roses will explode then gulp
to dust, and towers jerk up
like fingers, counting.
Throughout all this we will wake up together –
crumple-faced, eyes pearled with sleep, grouchy
or thirsting for tea or juice, or you will finger
these breasts until they raise up pips,
stir me where I blizzard and yolk,
make a bead of me;
have me call this pillow to a sour mash.
You will squash me against you when I'm crying like the rain,
croon and comfort. And for you I'll do the same.
Whilst the world wars, darling, such things will stay certain –
these fingers that thread your woolly chest,
this jumble of legs, this nest,
this waking to light and ourselves.

CHARLES DARWIN

Note on Marriage

This is the question

Mary

Children — (if it Please God) — Constant companion, (& friend in old age) who will feel interested in one, — object to be beloved & played with. — — better than a dog anyhow. — Home, & someone to take care of house — Charms of music & female chit-chat. — These things good for one's health. — *but terrible loss of time.* —

My God, it is intolerable to think of spending one's whole life, like a neuter bee, working, working, & nothing after all. — No, no won't do. — Imagine living all one's day solitarily in smoky dirty London House. — Only picture to yourself a nice soft wife on a sofa with good fire, & books & music perhaps — Compare this vision with the dingy reality of Grt. Marlbro' St.

Marry — Marry — Marry Q.E.D.

Not Mary

No children, (no second life), no one to care for one in old age.— What is the use of working 'in' without sympathy from near & dear friends—who are near & dear friends to the old, except relatives

Freedom to go where one liked — choice of Society & *little of it.* — Conversation of clever men at clubs — Not forced to visit relatives, & to bend in every trifle. — to have the expense & anxiety of children — perhaps quarelling — Loss of time. — cannot read in the Evenings — fatness & idleness — Anxiety & responsibility — less money for books &c — if many children forced to gain one's bread. — (But then it is very bad for one's health to work too much)

Perhaps my wife won't like London; then the sentence is banishment & degradation into indolent, idle fool —

MICHAEL LONGLEY

No Continuing City

*For here we have no continuing city... Saint Paul
to the Hebrews*

My hands here, gentle where her breasts begin,
My picture in her eyes –
It is time for me to recognise
This new dimension, my last girl.
So, to set my house in order, I imagine
Photographs, advertisements – the old lies,
The lumber of my soul –

All that is due for spring cleaning,
Everything that soul-destroys.
Into the open I bring
Girls who linger still in photostat
(For whom I was so many different boys)
I explode their myths before it is too late,
Their promises I detonate. –

There is quite a lot that I can do ...
I leave them – are they six or seven, two or three? –
Locked in their small geographies.
The hillocks of their bodies' lovely shires
(Whose all weathers I have walked through)
Acre by acre recede entire
To summer country.

From collision to eclipse their case is closed.
Who took me by surprise
Like comets first – now, failing to ignite,
They constellate such uneventful skies,
Their stars arranged each night
In the old stories
Which I successfully have diagnosed.

Though they momentarily survive
In my delays,
They neither cancel nor improve
My continuing city with old ways,
Familiar avenues to love –
Down my one way streets (it is time to finish)
Their eager syllables diminish.

Though they call out from the suburbs
Of experience – they know how that disturbs! –
Or, already tending towards home,
Prepare to hitch-hike on the kerbs,
Their bags full of dear untruths –
I am their medium
And take the words out of their mouths.

From today new hoardings crowd my eyes,
Pasted over my ancient histories
Which (I must be cruel to be kind)
Only gale or cloudburst now discover,
Ripping the billboard of my mind –
Oh, there my lovers,
There my dead no longer advertise.

I transmit from the heart a closing broadcast
To my girl, my bride, my wife-to be –
I tell her she is welcome,
Advising her to make this last,
To be sure of finding room in me
(I embody bed and breakfast) –
To eat and drink me out of house and home.

W. B. YEATS

He Wishes for the Cloths of Heaven

Had I the heavens' embroidered cloths,
Enwrought with golden and silver light,
The blue and the dim and the dark cloths
Of night and light and the half-light,
I would spread the cloths under your feet:
But I, being poor, have only my dreams;
I have spread my dreams under your feet;
Tread softly because you tread on my dreams.

DEREK MAHON

Preface to a Love Poem

This is a circling of itself and you—
A form of words, compact and compromise,
Prepared in the false dawn of the half-true
Beyond which the shapes of truth materialise.
This is a blind with sunlight filtering through.

This is a stirring in the silent hours,
As lovers do with thoughts they cannot frame
Or leave, but bring to darkness like night-flowers,
Words never choosing but the words choose them—
Birds crowing, wind whistling off pale stars.

This is a night-cry, neither here nor there,
A ghostly echo from the clamorous dead
Who cried aloud in anger and despair
Outlasting stone and bronze, but took instead
Their lost grins underground with them for ever.

This is at one remove, a substitute
For final answers; but the wise man knows
To cleave to the one living absolute
Beyond paraphrase, and shun a shrewd repose.
The words are aching in their own pursuit

To say 'l love you' out of indolence
As one might speak at sea without forethought,
Drifting inconsequently among islands.
This is a way of airing my distraught
Love of your silence; you are the soul of silence.

GERARD MANLEY HOPKINS

Epithalamion

Hark, hearer, hear what I do; lend a thought now, make
    believe
We are leaf–whelmed somewhere with the hood
Of some branchy bunchy bushybowered wood,
Southern dean or Lancashire clough or Devon cleave,
That leans along the loins of hills, where a candycoloured,
    where a gluegold-brown
Marbled river, boisterously beautiful, between
Roots and rocks is danced and dandled, all in froth and water-
    blowballs, down.
We are there, when we hear a shout
That the hanging honeysuck, the dogeared hazels in the cover
Makes dither, makes hover
And the riot of a rout
Of, it must be, boys from the town
Bathing: it is summer's sovereign good.

By there comes a listless stranger: beckoned by the noise
He drops towards the river: unseen
Sees the bevy of them, how the boys
With dare and with downdolphinry and bellbright bodies
    huddling out,
Are earthworld, airworld, waterworld thorough hurled, all by
    turn and turn about.

This garland of their gambol flashes in his breast
Into such a sudden zest
Of summertime joys
That he hies to a pool neighbouring; sees it is the best
There; sweetest, freshest, shadowiest;
Fairyland; silk-beech, scrolled ash, packed sycamore, wild
    wychelm, hornbeam fretty overstood
By. Rafts and rafts of flake leaves light, dealt so, painted on the
    air,
Hang as still as hawk or hawkmoth, as the stars or as the
    angels there,
Like the thing that never knew the earth, never off roots
Rose. Here he feasts: lovely all is! Nó more: off with—down
    he dings
His bleachèd both and woolwoven wear:
Careless these in coloured wisp
All lie tumbled-to; then with loop-locks
Forward falling, forehead frowning, lips crisp
Over finger-teasing task, his twiny boots
Fast he opens, last he off wrings
Till walk the world he can with bare his feet
And come where lies a coffer, burly all of blocks
Built of chancequarrièd, selfquainèd hoar-huskèd rocks
And the water warbles over into, filleted with glassy grassy
    quicksilvery shivès and shoots
And with heavenfallen freshness down from moorland still
    brims,
Dark or daylight on and on. Here he will then, here he will
    the fleet
Flinty kindcold element let break across his limbs
Long. Where we leave him, froliclavish while he looks about
    him, laughs, swims.

Enough now; since the sacred matter that I mean
I should be wronging longer leaving it to float
Upon this only gambolling and echoing-of-earth note—
What is … the delightful dean?
Wedlock. What the water? Spousal love.

....

....

Father, mother, brothers, sisters, friends
Into fairy trees, wildflowers, woodferns
Rankèd round the bower

....

OWEN SHEERS

Song

If we were magpies love,
and some day a bright bait caught your eye
and you were taken in a magpie trap,

a siren in a cage, then I would stay,
perch above you, spread my wings in the rain
and fan you with my feathers in the sun.

And when the others came,
drawn by the oil spill of your plumage,
the darkness of your eye,

I'd watch them strut in,
squawking to their doom
to find themselves trapped.

All night I'd listen to their confusion,
the beat of wing on wire, until the morning
and the farmer came to wring their lives away.

And through the winter I would feed you,
dropping the mites like kisses to your beak.
And in the Spring I'd sing, touch my wings to yours

while we waited for that day
when the farmer, realising at last as all men must
that love is all there is to save,

will open the door to your cage
and let you walk out to me,
where I will be waiting
to help you try your wings again.

EDWARD LEAR

The Owl and the Pussy-Cat

I

The Owl and the Pussy-Cat went to sea
   In a beautiful pea-green boat,
They took some honey, and plenty of money,
   Wrapped up in a five-pound note.
The Owl looked up to the stars above,
   And sang to a small guitar,
'O lovely Pussy, O Pussy, my love,
   What a beautiful Pussy you are,
      You are,
      You are!
What a beautiful Pussy you are!'

II

Pussy said to the Owl, 'You elegant fowl!
   How charmingly sweet you sing!
O let us be married! too long we have tarried:
   But what shall we do for a ring?'
They sailed away, for a year and a day,
   To the land where the Bong-tree grows
And there in a wood a Piggy-wig stood
   With a ring at the end of his nose,
      His nose,
      His nose,
With a ring at the end of his nose.

III

'Dear Pig, are you willing to sell for one shilling
  Your ring?' Said the Piggy, 'I will.'
So they took it away, and were married next day
  By the Turkey who lives on the hill.
They dined on mince, and slices of quince,
  Which they ate with a runcible spoon;
And hand in hand, on the edge of the sand,
  They danced by the light of the moon,
    The moon,
    The moon,
They danced by the light of the moon.

LOUIS MACNEICE

from *Trilogy for X*

When clerks and navvies fondle
    Beside canals their wenches,
In rapture or in coma
    The haunches that they handle,
And the orange moon sits idle
    Above the orchard slanted —
Upon such easy evenings
    We take our loves for granted.

But when, as now, the creaking
    Trees on the hills of London
Like bison charge their neighbours
    In wind that keeps up waking
And in the draught the scalloped
    Lampshade swings a shadow,
We think of love bound over —
    The mortgage on the meadow.

And one lies lonely, haunted
    By limbs he half remembers,
And one, in wedlock, wonders
    Where is the girl he wanted;
And some sit smoking, flicking

The ash away and feeling
For love gone up like vapour
    Between the floor and ceiling.

But now when winds are curling
    The trees do you come closer,
Close as an eyelid fasten
    My body in the darkness, darling;
Switch the light off and let me
    Gather you up and gather
The power of trains advancing
    Further, advancing further.

ANTON CHEKHOV

from The Proposal

Translated by Constance Garnett

Drawing-room in TCHUBUKOV's *house.* TCHUBUKOV *and* LOMOV; *the latter enters wearing evening dress and white gloves.*

TCHUBUKOV *(going to meet him).* My darling, whom do I see? Ivan Vassilyevitch! Delighted! [*Shakes hands.*] Well, this is a surprise, my dearie ... How are you?

LOMOV. I thank you. And pray, how are you?

TCHUBUKOV. We are getting on all right, thanks to your prayers, my angel, and all the rest of it. Please sit down ... It's too bad, you know, to forget your neighbours, darling. But, my dear, why this ceremoniousness? A swallow-tail, gloves, and all the rest of it! Are you going visiting, my precious?

LOMOV. No, I have only come to see you, honoured Stepan Stepanovitch.

TCHUBUKOV. Then why the swallow-tail, my charmer? As though you were paying calls on New Year's Day!

LOMOV. You see, this is how it is [*takes his arm*]. I have come, honoured Stepan Stepanovitch, to trouble you with a request. I have more than once had the honour of asking for your assistance, and you have always, so to speak – but pardon me, I am agitated. I will have a drink of water, honoured Stepan Stepanovitch [*drinks water*].

TCHUBUKOV [*aside*]. Come to ask for money! I am not going to give it to him. [*To him*] What is it, my beauty?

LOMOV. You see, Honour Stepanovitch – I beg pardon, Stepan

Honouritch … I am dreadfully agitated, as you see. In short, no one but you can assist me, though, of course, I have done nothing to deserve it, and … and … have no right to reckon upon your assistance …

TCHUBUKOV. Oh, don't spin it out, dearie. Come to the point. Well?

LOMOV. Immediately – in a moment. The fact is that I have come to ask for the hand of your daughter, Natalya Stepanovna.

TCHUBUKOV [*joyfully*]. You precious darling! Ivan Vassilyevitch, say it again! I can't believe my ears.

LOMOV. I have the honour to ask …

TCHUBUKOV [*interrupting*]. My darling! I am delighted, and all the rest of it. Yes, indeed, and all that sort of thing [*embraces and kisses him*]. I have been hoping for it for ages. It has always been my wish [*sheds a tear*]. And I have always loved you, my angel, as though you were my own son. God give you both love and good counsel, and all the rest of it. I have always wished for it … Why am I standing here like a post? I'm stupefied with joy, absolutely stupefied! Oh, from the bottom of my heart … I'll go and call Natasha and that sort of thing.

LOMOV [*touched*]. Honoured Stepan Stepanovitch, what do you think? May I hope that she will accept me?

TCHUBUKOV. A beauty like you, and she not accept you! I'll be bound she is as love-sick as a cat, and all the rest of it… In a minute! [*goes out.*]

ROBERT LOUIS STEVENSON

On Falling in Love
from Virginibus Puerisque

There is only one event in life which really astonishes a man and startles him out of his prepared opinions. Everything else befalls him very much as he expected. Event succeeds to event, with an agreeable variety indeed, but with little that is either startling or intense; they form together no more than a sort of background, or running accompaniment to the man's own reflections; and he falls naturally into a cool, curious, and smiling habit of mind, and builds himself up in a conception of life which expects tomorrow to be after the pattern of today and yesterday. He may be accustomed to the vagaries of his friends and acquaintances under the influence of love. He may sometimes look forward to it for himself with an incomprehensible expectation. But it is a subject in which neither intuition nor the behaviour of others will help the philosopher to the truth.

…When at last the scales fall from his eyes, it is not without something of the nature of dismay that the man finds himself in such changed conditions. He has to deal with commanding emotions instead of the easy dislikes and preferences in which he has hitherto passed his days; and he recognises capabilities for pain and pleasure of which he had not yet suspected the existence. Falling in love is the one illogical adventure, the one thing of which we are tempted to think as supernatural, in our trite and reasonable world. The effect is out of all proportion with the cause. Two persons, neither of them, it may be, very amiable or very beautiful, meet, speak a little, and look a little into each other's eyes. That has been done a dozen or so of times in the experience of either with no great result. But on this occasion all is different. They fall at once into that state in which another person becomes to us the very gist and centrepoint of God's creation, and demolishes our laborious theories with a smile; in which our ideas are so bound up with the one master-thought that even the trivial cares of our own person become so many acts of devotion, and the love of life itself is translated into a wish to remain in the same world with so precious and desirable a fellow-creature. And all the while their acquaintances look on in stupor, and ask each other, with almost passionate emphasis, what so-and-so can see in that woman, or such-an-one in that man? I am sure, gentlemen, I cannot tell you. For my part, I cannot think what the women mean. It might be very well, if the Apollo Belvedere should suddenly glow all over into life, and step forward from the pedestal with that godlike air of his. But of the misbegotten changelings who call themselves men, and prate intolerably over dinner-tables, I never saw one who seemed worthy to inspire love – no, nor read of any, except Leonardo da Vinci, and perhaps Goethe in his youth. About women I entertain a somewhat different opinion; but there, I have the misfortune to be a man.

JOHN MILTON

Song on May Morning

Now the bright morning Star, Dayes harbinger,
Comes dancing from the East, and leads with her
The Flowry *May*, who from her green lap throws
The yellow Cowslip, and the pale Primrose.
   Hail bounteous *May* that dost inspire
   Mirth and youth, and warm desire,
   Woods and Groves are of thy dressing,
   Hill and Dale doth boast thy blessing.
Thus we salute thee with our early Song,
And welcom thee, and wish thee long.

ALFRED, LORD TENNYSON

Marriage Morning

Light, so low upon earth,
　　You send a flash to the sun.
Here is the golden close of love,
　　All my wooing is done.
Oh, the woods, and the meadows,
　　Woods, where we hid from the wet,
Stiles where we stayed to be kind,
　　Meadows in which we met!
Light, so low in the vale
　　You flash and lighten afar,
For this is the golden morning of love,
　　And you are his morning star.
Flash, I am coming, I come,
　　By meadow and stile and wood,
Oh, lighten into my eyes and heart,
　　Into my heart and my blood!
Heart, are you great enough
　　For a love that never tires?
O heart, are you great enough for love?
　　I have heard of thorns and briers.
Over the thorns and briers,
　　Over the meadow and stiles,
Over the world to the end of it
　　Flash for a million miles.

DORIS LESSING

from The Pit

Once upon a time, when young, walking along a pavement or into a room, they had never failed to see in the faces turned towards them the gratified look that comes from absolute rightness. They had been a match, a pair, flesh of an immediately recognisable category of flesh. Both good-looking, healthy , fitted to mate and beget, causing none of the secret unease that people feel when confronted by couples who can make you think only of the unhealthy or ugly offspring they are likely to produce. Sarah and James had given others pleasure that had in fact little to do with being young handsome healthy and so on. No, it was because of their being flesh and one flesh. They had both been tall; she, slim, he, spare. Both were fair, he with shaggy Viking locks, she with long pale gleaming tresses. Both had very blue eyes, full of shrewd innocence. If there ever had been moments of disquiet in their early days, it was because of this: when they lay in each other's arms and looked into that other face, what they saw was so similar to what they saw in mirrors.

GERARD MANLEY HOPKINS

At the Wedding March

God with honour hang your head,
Groom, and grace you, bride, your bed
With lissome scions, sweet scions,
Out of hallowed bodies bred.

Each by other's comfort kind:
Déep, déeper than divined,
Divine charity, dear charity,
Fast you ever, fast bind.

Then let the march tread our ears:
I to him turn with tears
Who to wedlock, his wonder wedlock,
Déals tríumph and immortal years.

CHRISTINA ROSSETTI

from *Monna Innominata:*
A Sonnet of Sonnets

Vien dietro a me e lascia dir le genti. Dante
Contando i casi della vita nostra. Petrarca

Many in aftertimes will say of you
'He loved her'– while of me what will they say?
   Not that I loved you more than just in play,
For fashion's sake as idle women do.
Even let them prate; who know not what we knew
   Of love and parting in exceeding pain,
   Of parting hopeless here to meet again,
Hopeless on earth, and heaven is out of view.
But by my heart of love laid bare to you,
   My love that you can make not void nor vain,
Love that foregoes you but to claim anew
   Beyond this passage of the gate of death,
I charge you at the Judgment make it plain
   My love of you was life and not a breath.

J.M BARRIE

'Come Away, Come Away!'
from Peter And Wendy

He tried to argue with Tink. 'You know you can't be my fairy, Tink, because I am a gentleman and you are a lady.'

To this Tink replied in these words, 'You silly ass,' and disappeared into the bathroom.

'She is quite a common fairy,' Peter explained apologetically; 'she is called Tinker Bell because she mends the pots and kettles.'

They were together in the armchair by this time, and Wendy plied him with more questions.

'If you do not live in Kensington Gardens now—'

'Sometimes I do still.'

'But where do you live mostly now?'

'With the lost boys.'

'Who are they?'

'They are children who fall out of their perambulators when the nurse is looking the other way. If they are not claimed in seven days they are sent far away to the Neverland to defray expenses. I'm captain.'

'What fun it must be!'

'Yes,' said cunning Peter, 'but we are rather lonely. You see we have no female companionship.'

'Are none of the others girls?'

'Oh no; girls, you know, are much too clever to fall out of their prams.'

This flattered Wendy immensely. 'I think,' she said, 'it is perfectly lovely the way you talk about girls; John there just despises us.'

For reply Peter rose and kicked John out of the bed, blankets and all; one kick. This seemed to Wendy rather forward for a first meeting, and she told him with spirit that he was not captain in her house. However, John continued to sleep so placidly on the floor that she allowed him to remain there. 'And I know you meant to be kind,' she said, relenting, 'so you may give me a kiss.'

For the moment she had forgotten his ignorance about kisses. 'I thought you would want it back,' he said a little bitterly, and offered to return her thimble.

'Oh dear,' said the nice Wendy, 'I don't mean a kiss, I mean a thimble.'

'What's that?'

'It's like this.' She kissed him.

'Funny!' said Peter gravely. 'Now I shall give you a thimble?'

'If you wish to,' said Wendy, keeping her head erect this time.

Peter thimbled her, and almost immediately she screeched. 'What is it, Wendy?'

'It was exactly as if someone were pulling my hair.'

'That must have been Tink. I never knew her so naughty before.'

And indeed Tink was darting about again, using offensive language.

KATHERINE SWIFT

Terce
from The Morville Hours

You can smell the spring even before it arrives, like a seafarer becalmed for months on the wide expanse of ocean, scenting land before he sees it. Caught unaware, stooping perhaps to collect milk from the step; one morning it is suddenly there, on the breeze, unmistakable after the long months of winter: a smell compounded of greenness and rain showers and damp earth.; a hint of balsam, a rumour of hyacinths – pregnant with the ghosts of flowers-to-be, like Flora's breath. The clock strikes, the sound reverberating across the Church Meadow like ripples of water in the Mor Brook. Nine o'clock on a spring morning. How can you resist? The village is quiet; husbands, wives, children all despatched to office or school; hum of early morning traffic silenced; scrunch of postman's foot on gravel been and gone. Leave the mail unopened, the milk where it stands on the step. Follow your nose into the garden.

The scents of February and March were, like the violets, shy: you had to get down on your hands and knees to snuffle up the honey scent of snowdrops or the mossy green scent of the first daffodils. But now the foxy stink of emerging crown imperials comes bowling over the hedges to greet you. There's the pungent smell of wild garlic leaves trodden underfoot, the smell of newly mown grass and warm compost heaps. It's as if the tipping of the sun past the equinox has tripped a switch – as if those few extra seconds of light, that extra degree or two of inclination, had made all the difference. The air pulses with the sugar-sweet scent of Siberian wallflowers, the vanilla of *Clematis armandii*, choisyas and daphnes. Pure sex. Rooted to the spot, plants cannot walk around and look for a mate. Instead, they pump out these naked messages of seduction. Come hither, come hither. And the bees are only too happy to oblige, burying themselves headfirst in the flowers, nuzzling deep, drunk with nectar …

For it is – of course – a love affair, this passion for one's garden, and the very smell intoxicates like the smell of a lover.

JOHN DONNE

The Sun Rising

     Busy old fool, unruly Sun,
      Why dost thou thus,
Through windows, and through curtains, call on us?
Must to thy motions lovers' seasons run?
     Saucy pedantic wretch, go chide
     Late school-boys and sour prentices,
  Go tell court-huntsmen that the king will ride,
  Call country ants to harvest offices;
Love, all alike, no season knows nor clime,
Nor hours, days, months, which are the rags of time.

     Thy beams so reverend, and strong
      Why shouldst thou think?
I could eclipse and cloud them with a wink,
But that I would not lose her sight so long.
     If her eyes have not blinded thine,
     Look, and to-morrow late tell me,
  Whether both th' Indias of spice and mine
  Be where thou left'st them, or lie here with me.
Ask for those kings whom thou saw'st yesterday,
And thou shalt hear, 'All here in one bed lay.'

     She's all states, and all princes I;
      Nothing else is;
Princes do but play us; compared to this,
All honour's mimic, all wealth alchemy.

Thou, Sun, art half as happy as we,
In that the world's contracted thus;
Thine age asks ease, and since thy duties be
To warm the world, that's done in warming us.
Shine here to us, and thou art everywhere;
This bed thy center is, these walls thy sphere.

JO SHAPCOTT

Muse

When I kiss you in all the folding places
of your body, you make that noise like a dog
dreaming, dreaming of the long runs he makes
in answer to some jolt to his hormones,
running across landfills, running, running
by tips and shorelines from the scent of too much,
but still going with head up and snout
in the air because he loves it all
and has to get away. I have to kiss deeper
and more slowly – your neck, your inner arm,
the neat creases under your toes, the shadow
behind your knee, the white angles of your groin –
until you fall quiet because only then
can I get the damned words to come into my mouth.

D.H LAWRENCE

from Sons and Lovers

When she was twenty-three years old, she met, at a Christmas party, a young man from the Erewash Valley. Morel was then twenty-seven years old. He was well set-up, erect, and very smart. He had wavy black hair that shone again, and a vigorous black beard that had never been shaved. His cheeks were ruddy, and his red, moist mouth was noticeable because he laughed so often and so heartily. He had that rare thing, a rich, ringing laugh. Gertrude Coppard had watched him, fascinated. He was so full of colour and animation, his voice ran so easily into comic grotesque, he was so ready and so pleasant with everybody. Her own father had a rich fund of humour, but it was satiric. This man's was different: soft, non-intellectual, warm, a kind of gambolling.

She herself was opposite. She had a curious, receptive mind which found much pleasure and amusement in listening to other folk. She was clever in leading folk to talk. She loved ideas, and was considered very intellectual. What she liked most of all was an argument on religion or philosophy or politics with some educated man. This she did not often enjoy. So she always had people tell her about themselves, finding her pleasure so.

In her person she was rather small and delicate, with a large brow, and dropping bunches of brown silk curls. Her blue eyes were very straight, honest, and searching. She had the beautiful hands of the Coppards. Her dress was always subdued. She wore dark blue silk, with a peculiar silver chain of silver scallops. This, and a heavy brooch of twisted gold, was her only ornament. She was still perfectly intact, deeply religious, and full of beautiful candour.

JANE AUSTEN

from Sense and Sensibility

Unaccountable, however, as the circumstances of his release might appear to the whole family, it was certain that Edward was free; and to what purpose that freedom would be employed was easily pre-determined by all; for after experiencing the blessings of *one* imprudent engagement, contracted without his mother's consent, as he had already done for more than four years, nothing less could be expected of him in the failure of *that*, than the immediate contraction of another.

His errand at Barton, in fact, was a simple one. It was only to ask Elinor to marry him; and considering that he was not altogether inexperienced in such a question, it might be strange that he should feel so uncomfortable in the present case as he really did, so much in need of encouragement and fresh air.

How soon he had walked himself into the proper resolution, however, how soon an opportunity of exercising it occurred, in what manner he expressed himself, and how he was received, need not be particularly told. This only need be said—that when they all sat down to table at four o'clock, about three hours after his arrival, he had secured his lady, engaged her mother's consent, and was not only in the rapturous profession of the lover, but, in the reality of reason and truth, one of the happiest of men. His situation indeed was more than commonly joyful. He had more than the ordinary triumph of accepted love to swell his heart, and raise his spirits. He was released, without any reproach to himself, from an entanglement which had long formed his misery, from a woman whom he had long ceased to love—and elevated at once to that security with another, which he must have thought of almost with despair, as soon as he had learnt to consider it with desire. He was brought, not from doubt or suspense, but from misery to happiness; and the change was openly spoken in such a genuine, flowing, grateful cheerfulness, as his friends had never witnessed in him before.

His heart was now open to Elinor—all its weaknesses, all its errors confessed—and his first boyish attachment to Lucy treated with all the philosophic dignity of twenty-four.

WILLIAM SHAKESPEARE

Act V, Scene 2
from As You Like It

ROSALIND: O, my dear Orlando, how it grieves me to see thee wear thy heart in a scarf!

ORLANDO: It is my arm.

ROSALIND: I thought thy heart had been wounded with the claws of a lion.

ORLANDO: Wounded it is, but with the eyes of a lady.

ROSALIND: Did your brother tell you how I counterfeited to swoon when he show'd me your handkerchief?

ORLANDO: Ay, and greater wonders than that.

ROSALIND: O, I know where you are: nay, 'tis true. There was never any thing so sudden but the fight of two rams and Caesar's thrasonical brag of 'I came, saw, and overcame:' for your brother and my sister no sooner met but they look'd; no sooner look'd but they lov'd; no sooner lov'd but they sigh'd; no sooner sigh'd but they ask'd one another the reason; no sooner knew the reason but they sought the remedy; and in these degrees have they made a pair of stairs to marriage, which they will climb incontinent, or else be incontinent before marriage: they are in the very wrath of love, and they will together; clubs cannot part them.

The Declarations

PAUL MULDOON

Sideman

I'll be the Road Runner
To your Wile E Coyote
I'll take you in my stride
I'll be a Sancho Panza
To your Don Quixote
Your ever faithful guide

I'll stand by you in the lists
With our market strategists
I'll be your sideman, baby,
I'll be by your side

I'll be a Keith Richards
To your Mick Jagger
Before he let things slide
I'll be Sears to your Roebuck
Before he took the headstaggers
And opened nationwide

I'll support you at Wembley
I may require some assembly
But I'll be your sideman, baby,
I'll be by your side

I'll be McCartney to your Lennon
Lenin to your Marx

Jerry to your Ben &
Lewis to your Clark
Burke to your Hare
James Bond to your Q
BooBoo to your Yogi Bear
Tigger to your Pooh
Trigger to your Roy Rogers
Roy to your Siegfried
Fagin to your Artful Dodger
I guess I'll let you take the lead

(*guitar solo*)

I'll be a Chingachgook
To your Leatherstocking
A blaze of fur and hide
Our shares consolidated
Out directorates interlocking
I'll be along for the ride

I'll be at Ticonderoga
I'll be there for you at yoga
I'll be your sideman, baby,
I'll be by your side

ANNE BRADSTREET

To My Dear and Loving Husband

If ever two were one, then surely we.
If ever man were loved by wife, then thee;
If ever wife was happy in a man,
Compare with me, ye women, if you can.
I prize thy love more than whole mines of gold,
Or all the riches that the East doth hold.
My love is such that rivers cannot quench,
Nor ought but love from thee, give recompence.
Thy love is such I can no way repay,
The heavens reward thee manifold, I pray.
Then while we live, in love let's so persever,
That when we live no more, we may live ever.

ROBERT LOUIS STEVENSON

My Wife

Trusty, dusky, vivid, true,
With eyes of gold and bramble-dew,
Steel-true and blade-straight,
The great artificer
Made my mate.

Honour, anger, valour, fire,
A love that life could never tire,
Death quench or evil stir;
The mighty master
Gave to her.

Teacher, tender, comrade, wife,
A fellow-farer true through life,
Heart-whole and soul-free
The august father
Gave to me.

KATHLEEN JAMIE

Duet

I am the music of the string duet
In the Métro, and my circumstances,
nowadays, are music too: travelling
the underground like women's scent, or happiness.
Again and again I discover that I love you
as we navigate round Châtelet
and hear once more the music. It's found its way
through passages to where I least expect,
and when you kiss me, floods me.
The trains come in, whine out again,
the platforms fill and empty:
a movement regular as your heart's
beat, mine as lively as the melody.

LEANNE O'SULLIVAN

Comrades

(*for Susan*)

My heart's saviour,
my best friend, hear my voice
though distance overwhelms
and you waver between instinct and science.

Allow memory to rule over mind, over matter,
believe we can go beyond any distance,
believe I can clasp your hands
when they do not know where to reach.

Remember how our eyes bridged our souls.
Remember the bridge,
that linked the days we endured.

OSCAR WILDE

To My Wife – with a Copy of My Poems

I can write no stately proem
As a prelude to my lay;
From a poet to a poem
  I would dare to say.

For if of these fallen petals
One to you seem fair,
Love will waft it till it settles
On your hair.

And when wind and winter harden
All the loveless land,
It will whisper of the garden,
You will understand.

GLYN MAXWELL

Stargazing

The night is fine and dry. It falls and spreads
the cold sky with a million opposites
that, for a moment, seem like a million souls
and soon, none, and then, for what seems a long time,
one. Then of course it spins. What is better to do
than string out over the infinite dead spaces
the ancient beasts and spearmen of the human
mind, and, if not the real ones, new ones?

But, try making them clear to one you love –
whoever is standing by you is one you love
when pinioned by the stars – you will find it quite
impossible, but like her more for thinking
she sees that constellation.

After the wave of pain, you will turn to her
and, in an instant, change the universe
to a sky you were glad you came outside to see.

This is the act of all the descended gods
of every age and creed: to weary of all
that never ends, to take a human hand,
and go back into the house.

DANA GIOIA

The Song

How shall I hold my soul that it
does not touch yours? How shall I lift
it over you to other things?
If it would only sink below
into the dark like some lost thing
or slumber in some quiet place
which did not echo your soft heart's beat.
But all that ever touched us – you and me –
touched us together
                                        like a bow
that from two strings could draw one voice.
On what instrument were we strung?
And to what player did we sing
our interrupted song?

(After Rilke)

EDWARD THOMAS

After You Speak

After you speak
And what you meant
Is plain,
My eyes
Meet yours that mean—
With your cheeks and hair—
Something more wise,
More dark,
And far different.
Even so the lark
Loves dust
And nestles in it
The minute
Before he must
Soar in lone flight
So far,
Like a black star
He seems—
A mote
Of singing dust
Afloat
Above,
That dreams
And sheds no light.
I know your lust
Is love.

THOMAS HARDY

The Dawn after the Dance

Here is your parents' dwelling with its curtained windows
    telling
Of no thought of us within it or of our arrival here;
Their slumbers have been normal after one day more of formal
Matrimonial commonplace and household life's mechanic gear.

I would be candid willingly, but dawn draws on so chillingly
As to render further cheerlessness intolerable now,
So I will not stand endeavouring to declare a day for severing,
But will clasp you just as always—just the olden love avow.

Through serene and surly weather we have walked the ways
    together,
And this long night's dance this year's end eve now finishes the
    spell;
Yet we dreamt us but beginning a sweet sempiternal spinning
Of a cord we have spun to breaking—too intemperately, too
    well.

Yes; last night we danced I know, Dear, as we did that year ago,
    Dear,
When a new strange bond between our days was formed, and
    felt, and heard;
Would that dancing were the worst thing from the latest to the
    first thing
That the faded year can charge us with; but what avails a word!

That which makes man's love the lighter and the woman's burn
no brighter
Came to pass with us inevitably while slipped the shortening
year...
And there stands your father's dwelling with its blind bleak
windows telling
That the vows of man and maid are frail as filmy gossamere.

GEORGE HERBERT

Love (III)

Love bade me welcome: yet my soul drew back,
    Guilty of dust and sin.
But quick-eyed Love, observing me grow slack
    From my first entrance in,
Drew nearer to me, sweetly questioning
    If I lacked anything.

'A guest,' I answered, 'worthy to be here':
    Love said, 'You shall be he.'
'I, the unkind, the ungrateful? ah my dear,
    I cannot look on thee.'
Love took my hand and smiling did reply,
    'Who made the eyes but I?'

'Truth, Lord, but I have marred them; let my shame
    Go where it doth deserve.'
'And know you not,' says Love, 'who bore the blame?'
    'My dear, then I will serve.'
'You must sit down,' says Love, 'and taste my meat':
    So I did sit and eat.

ANNE LYNCH BOTTA

The Lake and Star

The mountain lake, o'ershadowed by the hills,
May still gaze heavenward on the evening star,
Whose distant light its dark recesses fills,
Though boundless distance must divide them far.
Still may the lake the star's bright image wear;
Still may the star, from its blue ether dome,
Shower down its silver beams across the gloom,
And light the wave that wanders darkly there.
Oh, my life's star! thus do I turn to thee
Amid the shadows that above me roll;
Thus from my distant sphere thou shin'st on me;
Thus does thine image float upon my soul,
Through the wide space that must our lives dissever,
Far as the lake and star, ah me! forever!

PHILIP LARKIN

Wedding Wind

The wind blew all my wedding-day,
And my wedding-night was the night of the high wind;
And a stable door was banging, again and again,
That he must go and shut it, leaving me
Stupid in candlelight, hearing rain,
Seeing my face in the twisted candlestick,
Yet seeing nothing. When he came back
He said the horses were restless, and I was sad
That any man or beast that night should lack
The happiness I had.
                                              Now in the day
All's ravelled under the sun by the wind's blowing.
He has gone to look at the floods, and I
Carry a chipped pail to the chicken-run,
Set it down, and stare. All is the wind
Hunting through clouds and forests, thrashing
My apron and the hanging cloths on the line.
Can it be borne, this bodying-forth by wind
Of joy my actions turn on, like a thread
Carrying beads? Shall I be let to sleep
Now this perpetual morning shares my bed?
Can even death dry up
These new delighted lakes, conclude
Our kneeling as cattle by all-generous waters?

COLE PORTER

Night and Day

Like the beat beat beat of the tom-tom
When the jungle shadows fall,
Like the tick tick tock of the stately clock
As it stands against the wall,

Like the drip drip drip of the raindrops
When the summer shower is through,
So a voice within me keeps repeating
You, you, you.

Night and day, you are the one.
Only you beneath the moon or under the sun.
Whether near to me, or far,
It's no matter, darling, where you are,
I think of you
Day and night, night and day, why is it so

That this longing for you follows wherever I go?
In the roaring traffic's boom
In the silence of my lonely room
I think of you
Day and night, night and day.

Under the hide of me
There's an oh such a hungry yearning burning inside of me,
And this torment won't be through
Until you let me spend my life making love to you
Day and night, night and day.

from The Prophet

Then Almitra spoke again and said, 'And what of Marriage,
    master?'
And he answered saying:
You were born together, and together you shall be for ever-
    more.
You shall be together when white wings of death scatter your
    days.
Aye, you shall be together even in the silent memory of God.
But let there be spaces in your togetherness,
And let the winds of the heavens dance between you.
Love one another but make not a bond of love:
Let it rather be a moving sea between the shores of your souls.
Fill each other's cup but drink not from one cup.
Give one another of your bread but eat not from the same loaf.
Sing and dance together and be joyous, but let each one of you
    be alone,
Even as the strings of a lute are alone though they quiver with
    the same music.
Give your hearts, but not into each other's keeping.
For only the hand of Life can contain your hearts.
And stand together, yet not too near together:
For the pillars of the temple stand apart,
And the oak tree and the cypress grow not in each other's
    shadow.

WILLIAM SHAKESPEARE

from *Venus and Adonis*

Love comforteth like sunshine after rain,
But Lust's effect is tempest after sun;
Love's gentle spring doth always fresh remain,
Lust's winter comes ere summer half be done;
Love surfeits not, Lust like a glutton dies;
Love is all truth, Lust full of forged lies.

FRANCES CORNFORD

The Avenue

Who has not seen their lover
Walking at ease,
Walking like any other
A pavement under trees,
Not singular, apart,
But footed, featured, dressed,
Approaching like the rest
In the same dapple of the summer caught;
Who has not suddenly thought
With swift surprise:
There walks in cool disguise,
There comes, my heart?

JOHN KEATS

Bright Star

Bright star, would I were steadfast as thou art –
Not in lone splendour hung aloft the night
And watching, with eternal lids apart,
Like nature's patient, sleepless Eremite,
The moving waters at their priestlike task
Of pure ablution round earth's human shores,
Or gazing on the new soft-fallen mask
Of snow upon the mountains and the moors—
No – yet still steadfast, still unchangeable,
Pillowed upon my fair love's ripening breast,
To feel for ever its soft swell and fall,
Awake for ever in a sweet unrest,
Still, still to hear her tender-taken breath,
And so live ever – or else swoon to death.

JOHN DONNE

The Ecstasy

Where, like a pillow on a bed,
   A pregnant bank swell'd up, to rest
The violet's reclining head,
   Sat we two, one another's best.

Our hands were firmly cemented
   By a fast balm, which thence did spring;
Our eye-beams twisted, and did thread
   Our eyes upon one double string.

So to engraft our hands, as yet
   Was all the means to make us one;
And pictures in our eyes to get
   Was all our propagation.

As, 'twixt two equal armies, Fate
   Suspends uncertain victory,
Our souls—which to advance their state,
   Were gone out—hung 'twixt her and me.

And whilst our souls negotiate there,
   We like sepulchral statues lay;
All day, the same our postures were,
   And we said nothing, all the day.

If any, so by love refined,
    That he soul's language understood,
And by good love were grown all mind,
    Within convenient distance stood,

He—though he knew not which soul spake,
    Because both meant, both spake the same—
Might thence a new concoction take,
    And part far purer than he came.

This ecstasy doth unperplex
    (We said) and tell us what we love;
We see by this, it was not sex;
    We see, we saw not, what did move:

But as all several souls contain
    Mixture of things they know not what,
Love these mix'd souls doth mix again,
    And makes both one, each this, and that.

A single violet transplant,
    The strength, the colour, and the size—
All which before was poor and scant—
    Redoubles still, and multiplies.

When love with one another so
    Interanimates two souls,
That abler soul, which thence doth flow,
    Defects of loneliness controls.

We then, who are this new soul, know,
  Of what we are composed, and made,
For th' atomies of which we grow
  Are souls, whom no change can invade.

But, O alas! so long, so far,
  Our bodies why do we forbear?
They are ours, though not we; we are
  Th'intelligences, they the spheres.

We owe them thanks, because they thus
  Did us, to us, at first convey,
Yielded their senses' force to us,
  Nor are dross to us, but allay.

On man heaven's influence works not so,
  But that it first imprints the air;
For soul into the soul may flow,
  Though it to body first repair.

As our blood labours to beget
  Spirits, as like souls as it can;
Because such fingers need to knit
  That subtle knot, which makes us man;

So must pure lovers' souls descend
  To affections, and to faculties,
Which sense may reach and apprehend,
  Else a great prince in prison lies.

To our bodies turn we then, that so
   Weak men on love reveal'd may look;
Love's mysteries in souls do grow,
   But yet the body is his book.

And if some lover, such as we,
   Have heard this dialogue of one,
Let him still mark us, he shall see
   Small change when we're to bodies gone.

THOMAS CAREW

Boldness in Love

Mark how the bashful morn in vain
Courts the amorous marigold,
With sighing blasts and weeping rain,
Yet she refuses to unfold.

But when the planet of the day
Approacheth with his powerful ray,
Then she spreads, then she receives
His warmer beams into her virgin leaves.

So shalt thou thrive in love, fond boy;
If thy sighs and tears discover
Thy grief, thou never shalt enjoy
The just reward of a bold lover.

But when with moving accents thou
Shalt constant faith and service vow,
Thy Celia shall receive those charms
With open ears, and with unfolded arms.

ADELAIDE ANNE PROCTER

Love in Mayfair

I must tell you, my dear,
   I'm in love with him, vastly!
Twenty thousand a year,
I must tell you, my dear!
He will soon be a peer –
   And such diamonds! – and, lastly,
I must tell you, my dear,
   I'm in love with him, vastly!

W.B. YEATS

A Poet to His Beloved

I bring you with reverent hands
The books of my numberless dreams,
White woman that passion has worn
As the tide wears the dove-grey sands,
And with heart more old than the horn
That is brimmed from the pale fire of time:
White woman with numberless dreams,
I bring you my passionate rhyme.

FYODOR DOSTOEVSKY

from White Nights

Translated by Constance Garnett

Thank you, yes, thank you for that love! For it will live in my memory like a sweet dream which lingers long after awakening; for I shall remember for ever that instant when you opened your heart to me like a brother and so generously accepted the gift of my shattered heart to care for it, nurse it, and heal it ... If you forgive me, the memory of you will be exalted by a feeling of everlasting gratitude which will never be effaced from my soul ... I will treasure that memory: I will be true to it, I will not betray it, I will not betray my heart: it is too constant.

RUDYARD KIPLING

My Lady's Law

The Law whereby my lady moves
Was never Law to me,
But 'tis enough that she approves
Whatever Law it be.

For in that Law, and by that Law,
My constant course I'll steer;
Not that I heed or deem it dread,
But that she holds it dear.

Tho' Asia sent for my content
Her richest argosies,
Those would I spurn, and bid return,
If that should give her ease.

With equal heart I'd watch depart
Each spicèd sail from sight,
Sans bitterness, desiring less
Great gear than her delight.

Though Kings made swift with many a gift
My proven sword to hire,
I would not go nor serve 'em so,
Except at her desire.

With even mind, I'd put behind
Adventure and acclaim,
And clean give o'er, esteeming more
Her favour than my fame.

Yet such am I, yea such am I—
Sore bond and freest free,
The Law that sways my lady's ways
Is mystery to me!

CAROL ANN DUFFY

Words, Wide Night

Somewhere on the other side of this wide night
and the distance between us, I am thinking of you.
The room is turning slowly away from the moon.

This is pleasurable. Or shall I cross that out and say
it is sad? In one of the tenses I singing
an impossible song of desire that you cannot hear.

La lala la. See? I close my eyes and imagine
the dark hills I would have to cross
to reach you. For I am in love with you and this

is what it is like or what it is like in words.

NICK LAIRD

Estimates

Who knows what you mean by love?
Extrapolating from the facts
you want two hundred friends
to watch
you wear the white and walk the aisle.

We could pack the car and motor north
to waterfall and rock, a nightfall
lit by moonlight on the snowfall
patches
still intact among the sheep tracks

and the turf-banks and the heather.
We could pull in somewhere there,
kill the engine, wait,
listen
to a late-night country music station,

split bars of dark and fruit-&-nut,
sip amaretto from the lid, skin up,
and wake,
unwashed and cramped
as man and wife

in a place unpeopled, dawn-calm,
cleared of its gestures, its features

by weather, to mountains,
and mountains of clouds.
We could.

MICHAEL ONDAATJE

The Cinnamon Peeler

If I were a cinnamon peeler
I would ride your bed
and leave the yellow bark dust
on your pillow.

Your breast and shoulders would reek
you could never walk through markets
without the profession of my fingers
floating over you. The blind would
stumble certain of whom they approached
though you might bathe
under rain gutters, monsoon.

Here on the upper thigh
at this smooth pasture
neighbour to your hair
or the crease
that cuts your back. This ankle.
You will be known among strangers
as the cinnamon peeler's wife.

I could hardly glance at you
before marriage
never touch you
– your keen-nosed mother, your rough brothers.
I buried my hands

in saffron, disguised them
over smoking tar,
helped the honey gatherers …

When we swam once
I touched you in water
and our bodies remained free,
you could hold me and be blind of smell.
You climbed the bank and said

                    this is how you touch other women
the grass cutter's wife, the lime burner's daughter
And you searched your arms
for the missing perfume

                    and knew

            what good it is
to be the lime burner's daughter
left with no trace
as if not spoken to in the act of love
as if wounded without the pleasure of a scar.

You touched
your belly to my hands
in the dry air and said
I am the cinnamon
peeler's wife. Smell me.

JOHN CLARE

Where She Told Her Love

I saw her crop a rose
Right early in the day,
And I went to kiss the place
Where she broke the rose away;
And I saw the patten rings
Where she o'er the stile had gone,
And I love all other things
Her bright eyes look upon.
If she looks upon the hedge or up the leafing tree,
The whitethorn or the brown oak are made dearer
   things to me.

I have a pleasant hill
Which I sit upon for hours,
Where she cropt some sprigs of thyme
And other little flowers;
And she muttered as she did it
As does beauty in a dream,
And I loved her when she hid it
On her breast, so like to cream,
Near the brown mole on her neck that to me a
   diamond shone;
Then my eye was like to fire, and my heart was like to
   stone.

There is a small green place
Where cowslips early curled,
Which on Sabbath days I traced,
The dearest in the world.
A little oak spreads o'er it,
And throws a shadow round,
A green sward close before it,
The greenest ever found:
There is not a woodland nigh nor is there a green
   grove,
Yet stood the fair maid nigh me and told me all her
   love.

HARTLEY COLERIDGE

Friendship

When we were idlers with the loitering rills,
The need of human love we little noted:
  Our love was nature; and the peace that floated
On the white mist, and dwelt upon the hills,
To sweet accord subdued our wayward wills:
  One soul was ours, one mind, one heart devoted,
  That, wisely doting, ask'd not why it doted,
And ours the unknown joy, which knowing kills.
  But now I find how dear thou wert to me;
  That man is more than half of nature's treasure,
Of that fair beauty which no eye can see,
  Of that sweet music which no ear can measure;
  And now the streams may sing for others' pleasure,
The hills sleep on in their eternity.

ELIZA ACTON

I Love Thee

I love thee, as I love the calm
   Of sweet, star-lighted hours!
I love thee, as I love the balm
   Of early jasmine flowers.

I love thee, as I love the last
   Rich smile of fading day,
Which lingereth, like the look we cast,
   On rapture pass'd away.

I love thee, as I love the tone
   Of some soft-breathing flute,
Whose soul is wak'd for me alone
   When all beside is mute.

I love thee, as I love the first
   Young violet of the spring;
Or the pale lily, April-nurs'd,
   To scented blossoming.

I love thee, as I love the full,
   Clear gushings of the song,
Which lonely, sad, and beautiful
   At night-fall floats along,

Pour'd by the bul-bul forth to greet
    The hours of rest and dew;
When melody and moonlight meet
    To blend their charm and hue.

I love thee, as the glad bird loves
    The freedom of its wing,
On which delightedly it moves
    In wildest wandering.

I love thee, as I love the swell,
    And hush, of some low strain,
Which bringeth, by its gentle spell,
    The past to life again.

Such is the feeling which from thee
    Naught earthly can allure:
'Tis ever link'd to all I see
    Of gifted — high – and pure!

SAMUEL TAYLOR COLERIDGE

from *Love*

All thoughts, all passions, all delights,
Whatever stirs this mortal frame,
Are all but ministers of Love,
   And feed his sacred flame.

Oft in my waking dreams do I
Live o'er again that happy hour,
When midway on the mount I lay
   Beside the ruined tower.

The moonshine stealing o'er the scene
Had blended with the lights of eve;
And she was there, my hope, my joy,
   My own dear Genevieve!

She leant against the armèd man,
The statue of the armèd knight;
She stood and listened to my lay,
   Amid the lingering light.

Few sorrows hath she of her own,
My hope! my joy! my Genevieve!
She loves me best, whene'er I sing
   The songs that make her grieve.

I played a soft and doleful air,
I sang an old and moving story –
An old rude song, that suited well
   That ruin wild and hoary.

She listened with a flitting blush,
With downcast eyes and modest grace;
For well she knew I could not choose
   But gaze upon her face.

I told her of the Knight that wore
Upon his shield a burning brand;
And that for ten long years he wooed
   The Lady of the Land.

I told her how he pined: and ah!
The deep, the low, the pleading tone
With which I sang another's love
   Interpreted my own.

She wept with pity and delight,
She blushed with love, and virgin shame;
And like the murmur of a dream,
   I heard her breathe my name.

. . . .

Her bosom heaved – she stepped aside,
As conscious of my look she stepped –
Then suddenly, with timorous eye,
   She fled to me and wept.

She half enclosed me with her arms,
She pressed me with a meek embrace;
And bending back her head, looked up,
 And gazed upon my face.

'Twas partly love, and partly fear,
And partly 'twas a bashful art,
That I might rather feel, than see,
 The swelling of her heart.

I calmed her fears, and she was calm,
And told her love with virgin pride;
And so I won my Genevieve,
 My bright and beauteous Bride.

WILLIAM SHAKESPEARE

Sonnet XXIX

When in disgrace with fortune and men's eyes,
I all alone beweep my outcast state,
And trouble deaf Heaven with my bootless cries,
And look upon myself, and curse my fate,
Wishing me like to one more rich in hope,
Featur'd like him, like him with friends possess'd,
Desiring this man's art, and that man's scope,
With what I most enjoy contented least:
Yet in these thoughts myself almost despising,
Haply I think on thee, —and then my state
(Like to the lark at break of day arising
From sullen earth) sings hymns at heaven's gate;
For thy sweet love remember'd such wealth brings
That then I scorn to change my state with kings'.

PAUL BATCHELOR

Pygmalion's Prayer to Venus

Once it was enough, more than enough,
to have your likeness carved in cedar; to kiss
your belly: cedar-gold; your shoulder: cedar-sweet.
Clear-eyed & kind, hear what I cannot say.

This careful likeness carved in cedar by
my journeyman hand looks well, but never well enough.
Clear-eyed & kind, hear all I dare not say:
your sympathetic magic knows

my journeyman heart too well, or well enough;
hear this sinner's prayer for flesh & blood.
Your sympathetic magic knows
I only ever worshipped you.

Grant my idiot wish for flesh & blood
and that will be enough, more than enough,
for one who only ever worshipped you,
your belly: cedar-gold; your shoulder: cedar-sweet...

WILLIAM SHAKESPEARE

Act II, Scene II
from Antony and Cleopatra

DOMITIUS ENOBARBUS:
  I will tell you.
  The barge she sat in, like a burnish'd throne,
  Burn'd on the water: the poop was beaten gold;
  Purple the sails, and so perfumed that
  The winds were love-sick with them; the oars were silver,
  Which to the tune of flutes kept stroke, and made
  The water which they beat to follow faster,
  As amorous of their strokes. For her own person,
  It beggar'd all description: she did lie
  In her pavilion – cloth-of-gold of tissue –
  O'er-picturing that Venus where we see
  The fancy outwork nature: on each side her
  Stood pretty dimpled boys, like smiling Cupids,
  With divers-colour'd fans, whose wind did seem
  To glow the delicate cheeks which they did cool,
  And what they undid did.

AGRIPPA:
  O, rare for Antony!

DOMITIUS ENOBARBUS:
  Her gentlewomen, like the Nereides,
  So many mermaids, tended her i' the eyes,
  And made their bends adornings: at the helm
  A seeming mermaid steers: the silken tackle

Swell with the touches of those flower-soft hands,
That yarely frame the office. From the barge
A strange invisible perfume hits the sense
Of the adjacent wharfs. The city cast
Her people out upon her; and Antony,
Enthroned i' the market-place, did sit alone,
Whistling to the air; which, but for vacancy,
Had gone to gaze on Cleopatra too,
And made a gap in nature.

The Vows

GEORGE HERBERT

A Wreath

A wreathed garland of deservèd praise,
Of praise deservèd, unto Thee I give,
I give to Thee, who knowest all my ways,
My crooked winding ways, wherein I live,
Wherein I die, not live; for life is straight,
Straight as a line, and ever tends to Thee,
To Thee, who art more far above deceit,
Than deceit seems above simplicity.
Give me simplicity, that I may live,
So live and like, that I may know Thy ways,
Know them and practise them: then shall I give
For this poor wreath, give Thee a crown of praise.

RICHARD WILBUR

A Wedding Toast

M.C.H.
C.H.W.
14 July 1971

St John tells how, at Cana's wedding-feast,
The water-pots poured wine in such amount
That by his sober count
there were a hundred gallons at the least.

It made no earthly sense, unless to show
How whatsoever love elects to bless
Brims to a sweet excess
That can without depletion overflow.

Which is to say that what love sees is true;
That the world's fullness is not made but found.
Life hungers to abound
And pour its plenty out for such as you.

Now, if your loves will lend an ear to mine,
I toast you both, good son and dear new daughter.
May you not lack for water,
And may that water smack of Cana's wine.

JOHN DONNE

from *Epithalamion Made At Lincoln's Inn*

I

The sun-beams in the east are spread;
Leave, leave, fair bride, your solitary bed;
   No more shall you return to it alone;
It nurseth sadness, and your body's print,
Like to a grave, the yielding down doth dint;
   You, and your other you, meet there anon.
   Put forth, put forth, that warm balm-breathing thigh,
Which when next time you in these sheets will smother,
   There it must meet another,
     Which never was, but must be, oft, more nigh.
Come glad from thence, go gladder than you came;
To-day put on perfection, and a woman's name.

Daughters of London, you which be
Our golden mines, and furnish'd treasury;
   You which are angels, yet still bring with you
Thousands of angels on your marriage days;
Help with your presence, and devise to praise
   These rites, which also unto you grow due;
   Conceitedly dress her, and be assign'd,
By you fit place for every flower and jewel;
   Make her for love fit fuel,
     As gay as Flora and as rich as Ind;

So may she, fair and rich in nothing lame,
To-day put on perfection, and a woman's name.

And you frolic patricians,
Sons of those senators, wealth's deep oceans;
   Ye painted courtiers, barrels of other's wits;
Ye countrymen, who but your beasts love none;
Ye of those fellowships, whereof he's one,
   Of study and play made strange hermaphrodites,
   Here shine ; this bridegroom to the temple bring.
Lo, in yon path which store of strew'd flowers graceth,
   The sober virgin paceth;
      Except my sight fail, 'tis no other thing.
Weep not, nor blush, here is no grief nor shame,
To-day put on perfection, and a woman's name.

Thy two-leaved gates, fair temple, unfold,
And these two in thy sacred bosom hold,
   Till mystically join'd but one they be;
Then may thy lean and hunger-starvèd womb
Long time expect their bodies, and their tomb,
   Long after their own parents fatten thee.
   All elder claims, and all cold barrenness,
All yielding to new loves, be far for ever,
   Which might these two dissever;
      Always, all th'other may each one possess;
For the best bride, best worthy of praise and fame,
To-day puts on perfection, and a woman's name.

RODDY LUMSDEN

On a Promise

(*an epithalamium*)

And if not caution, then its conduit
Is given to the wind. A giddy ship
Of fools and family, rocking loose (to wit,

There's drink and dancing) witness as you slip
The foolish purchase freedom had become.
Then, clutching at complexity, we strip

The willow, strange brutes turning in a hum
Of shuttles, stripped of any code of dress,
And swirling girls who gracefully succumb

To gallivanting into breathlessness.
And in complexity, accessory
To a loom more excessive than this mess

We mimics weave on, a promissory
Rationale emerges (and not by chance
There's method in this), a necessary

Arrangement we have conjured from the dance
To celebrate that promises are made
And bargained down, from bittersweet advance

To oath of no retreat, that best schemes laid
To last still can, to scold the cynic's tongue.
No one would claim the tune won't be replayed,

That other hearts won't race, bells hang unrung,
But such shapes aren't fashioned to go through
A repetition. Something is begun

Some things are made just once, and made for you.

G.K CHESTERTON

A Defense of Rash Vows
from The Defendant

But what have lovers to do with ridiculous affectations of fearing no man or woman? They know that in the turning of a hand the whole cosmic engine to the remotest star may become an instrument of music or an instrument of torture. They hear a song older than Suckling's, that has survived a hundred philosophies. 'Who is this that looketh out of the window, fair as the sun, clear as the moon, terrible as an army with banners?'

As we have said, it is exactly this backdoor, this sense of having a retreat behind us, that is, to our minds, the sterilising spirit in modern pleasure. Everywhere there is the persistent and insane attempt to obtain pleasure without paying for it. Thus, in politics the modern Jingoes practically say, 'Let us have the pleasures of conquerors without the pains of soldiers: let us sit on sofas and be a hardy race.' Thus, in religion and morals, the decadent mystics say: 'Let us have the fragrance of sacred purity without the sorrows of self-restraint; let us sing hymns alternately to the Virgin and Priapus.' Thus in love the free-lovers say: 'Let us have the splendour of offering ourselves without the peril of committing ourselves; let us see whether one cannot commit suicide an unlimited number of times.'

Emphatically it will not work. There are thrilling moments, doubtless, for the spectator, the amateur, and the aesthete; but there is one thrill that is known only to the soldier who fights for his own flag, to the ascetic who starves himself for his own illumination, to the lover who makes finally his own choice. And it is this transfiguring self-discipline that makes the vow a truly sane thing. It must have satisfied even the giant hunger of the soul of a lover or a poet to know that in consequence of some one instant of decision that strange chain would hang for centuries in the Alps among the silences of stars and snows. All around us is the city of small sins, abounding in backways and retreats, but surely, sooner or later, the towering flame will rise from the harbour announcing that the reign of the cowards is over and a man is burning his ships.

SIR PHILIP SIDNEY

The Bargain

My true love hath my heart, and I have his,
    By just exchange one for another given:
I hold his dear, and mine he cannot miss,
    There never was a better bargain driven:
My true love hath my heart, and I have his.

His heart in me keeps him and me in one,
    My heart in him his thoughts and senses guides:
He loves my heart, for once it was his own,
    I cherished his because in me it bides:
My true love hath my heart, and I have his.

W. B. YEATS

A Drinking Song

Wine comes in at the mouth
And love comes in at the eye;
That's all we shall know for truth
Before we grow old and die.
I lift the glass to my mouth,
I look at you, and I sigh.

CAITRIONA O'REILLY

Possession

That anxious way you have of closing doors
(like the brown of your hair and eyes)
was never really yours.
My arms and elongated nose were owned before –
fragments of jigsaw
in the rough art assemblage whose end we are.

Sometimes I don't know where we live
or whose voice I still
hear and remember
inside my head at night. In darkness and in love
we are dismembered,
so that the fact of our coming to at all

becomes a morning miracle. Let's number
our fingers and toes again.
Do I love you piecemeal
when I see in your closing hand a valve-flower
like a sea-anemone,
or is it our future I remember, as the White Queen

remembered her pinpricked finger? All of you
that's to be known
resides in that small gesture.

And though our days consist of letting go –
since neither one can own
the other – what still deepens pulls us back together.

GEORGE HERBERT

Love (II)

Immortall Heat, O let Thy greater flame
   Attract the lesser to it: let those fires
   Which shall consume the world, first make it tame,
And kindle in our hearts such true desires,

As may consume our lusts, and make Thee way.
   Then shall our hearts pant Thee; then shall our brain
   All her invention on Thine altar lay,
And there in hymnes send back Thy fire again:

Our eies shall see Thee, which before saw dust;
   Dust blown by Wit, till that they both were blinde:
   Thou shalt recover all thy goods in kinde,
Who wert disseized by usurping lust:

   All knees shall bow to thee; all wits shall rise,
   And praise Him who did make and mend our eies.

THOMAS CAREW

Eternity of Love Protested

How ill doth he deserve a lover's name
    Whose pale weak flame
    Cannot retain
His heat, in spite of absence or disdain;
But doth at once, like paper set on fire,
    Burn and expire!
True love can never change his seat,
Nor did he ever love that could retreat.

That noble flame, which my breast keeps alive,
    Shall still survive
    When my soul's fled;
Nor shall my love die, when my body's dead;
That shall wait on me to the lower shade,
    And never fade.
My very ashes in their urn
Shall, like a hallow'd lamp, for ever burn.

WILLIAM MORRIS

Love is Enough

Love is enough: though the World be a-waning,
And the woods have no voice but the voice of complaining,
  Though the sky be too dark for dim eyes to discover
The gold-cups and daisies fair blooming thereunder,
Though the hills be held shadows, and the sea a dark wonder,
 And this day draw a veil over all deeds pass'd over,
Yet their hands shall not tremble, their feet shall not falter;
The void shall not weary, the fear shall not alter
  These lips and these eyes of the loved and the lover.

JOHN FLETCHER

To Venus

Oh, fair sweet goddess, queen of loves,
Soft and gentle as thy doves,
Humble-eyed, and ever ruing
Those poor hearts, their loves pursuing!
Oh, thou mother of delights,
Crowner of all happy nights,
Star of dear content and pleasure,
Of mutual loves and endless treasure!
Accept this sacrifice we bring,
Thou continual youth and spring;
Grant this lady her desires,
And every hour we'll crown thy fires.

JAMES FENTON

Hinterhof

Stay near to me and I'll stay near to you –
As near as you are dear to me will do,
    Near as the rainbow to the rain,
    The west wind to the windowpane,
As fire to the hearth, as dawn to dew.

Stay true to me and I'll stay true to you –
As true as you are new to me will do,
    New as the rainbow in the spray,
    Utterly new in every way,
New in the way that what you say is true.

Stay near to me, stay true to me. I'll stay
As near, as true to you as heart could pray.
    Heart never hoped that one might be
    Half of the things you are to me –
The dawn, the fire, the rainbow, and the day.

MARY ROBINSON

from Sappho and Phaon

XIII She Endeavours to Fascinate Him

Bring, bring to deck my brow, ye Sylvan girls,
A roseate wreath; nor for my waving hair
The costly band of studded gems prepare,
Of sparkling chrysolite or orient pearls:
Love, o'er my head his canopy unfurls,
His purple pinions fan the whisp'ring air;
Mocking the golden sandal, rich and rare,
Beneath my feet the fragrant woodbine curls.
Bring the thin robe, to fold about my breast,
White as the downy swan; while round my waist
Let leaves of glossy myrtle bind the vest,
Not idly gay, but elegantly chaste!
Love scorns the nymph in wanton trappings drest;
And charms the most conceal'd, are doubly grac'd.

XX To Phaon

Oh! I could toil for thee o'er burning plains;
Could smile at poverty's disastrous blow;
With thee, could wander 'midst a world of snow,
Where one long night o'er frozen Scythia reigns.
Sever'd from thee, my sick'ning soul disdains

The thrilling thought, the blissful dream to know,
And can'st thou give my days to endless woe,
Requiting sweetest bliss with cureless pains?
Away, false fear! nor think capricious fate
Would lodge a daemon in a form divine!
Sooner the dove shall seek a tyger mate,
Or the soft snow-drop round the thistle twine;
Yet, yet, I dread to hope, nor dare to hate,
Too proud to sue! too tender to resign!

ANNE LYNCH BOTTA

The Sun and Stream

As some dark stream within a cavern's breast,
Flows murmuring, moaning, for the distant sun,
So ere I met thee, murmuring its unrest,
Did my life's current coldly, darkly, run.
And as that stream, beneath the sun's full gaze,
Its separate course and life no more maintains,
But now absorbed, transfused far o'er the plains,
It floats, etherealised in those warm rays;
So in the sunlight of thy fervid love,
My heart, so long to earth's dark channels given,
Now soars, all pain, all doubt, all ill above,
And breathes the ether of the upper Heaven;
So thy high spirit holds and governs mine;
So is my life, my being, lost in thine!

JOHN DONNE

Love's Growth

I scarce believe my love to be so pure
      As I had thought it was,
      Because it doth endure
Vicissitude, and season, as the grass;
Methinks I lied all winter, when I swore
My love was infinite, if spring make it more.

But if this medicine, love, which cures all sorrow
    With more, not only be no quintessence,
    But mix'd of all stuffs, vexing soul, or sense,
And of the sun his active vigour borrow,
Love's not so pure, and abstract as they use
To say, which have no mistress but their Muse;
But as all else, being elemented too,
Love sometimes would contemplate, sometimes do.

And yet no greater, but more eminent,
      Love by the spring is grown;
      As in the firmament
Stars by the sun are not enlarged, but shown,
Gentle love deeds, as blossoms on a bough,
From love's awakened root do bud out now.

If, as in water stirr'd more circles be
    Produced by one, love such additions take,
    Those like so many spheres but one heaven make,

For they are all concentric unto thee;
And though each spring do add to love new heat,
As princes do in times of action get
New taxes, and remit them not in peace,
No winter shall abate this spring's increase.

LOUIS DE BERNIÈRES

from Captain Corelli's Mandolin

'Love is a temporary madness, it erupts like volcanoes and then subsides. And when it subsides, you have to make a decision. You have to work out whether your roots have so entwined together that it is inconceivable that you should ever part. Because this is what love is. Love is not breathlessness, it is not excitement, it is not the promulgation of promises of eternal passion, it is not the desire to mate every second minute of the day, it is not lying awake at night imagining that he is kissing every cranny of your body. No, don't blush, I am telling you some truths. That is just being "in love", which any fool can do. Love itself is what is left over when being in love has burned away, and this is both an art and a fortunate accident.'

THOMAS LOVELL BEDDOES

Song

Bride:
How many times do I love thee, dear?
  Tell me how many thoughts there be
    In the atmosphere
    Of a new-fall'n year,
Whose white and sable hours appear
  The latest flake of Eternity:
So many times do I love thee, dear.

Groom:
How many times do I love again?
  Tell me how many beads there are
    In a silver chain
    Of evening rain,
Unravelled from the tumbling main,
  And threading the eye of a yellow star;
So many times do I love again.

WILLIAM SHAKESPEARE

Sonnet LXXV

So are you to my thoughts as food to life,
Or as sweet-season'd showers are to the ground;
And for the peace of you I hold such strife
As 'twixt a miser and his wealth is found;
Now proud as an enjoyer, and anon
Doubting the filching age will steal his treasure;
Now counting best to be with you alone,
Then better'd that the world may see my pleasure;
Sometime all full with feasting on your sight,
And by and by clean starvèd for a look;
Possessing or pursuing no delight
Save what is had, or must from you be took.
   Thus do I pine and surfeit day by day,
   Or gluttoning on all, or all away.

Quaker Wedding Vow

i.

In the presence of God, Friends, I take this my friend [name]to be my husband, promising, through divine assistance, to be unto him a loving and faithful wife, so long as we both on earth shall live.

ii.

In the fear of the Lord and in the presence of this assembly, Friends, I take this my friend [name] to be my wife, promising, with God's help to be unto her a loving and faithful husband, until it shall please the Lord by death to separate us.

Roman Catholic Vows

I, ____, take you, ____, to be my [husband/wife]. I promise to be true to you in good times and in bad, in sickness and in health. I will love you and honour you all the days of my life.

I, ____, take you, ____, for my lawful [husband/wife], to have and to hold, from this day forward, for better, for worse, for richer, for poorer, in sickness and in health, until death do us part.

The priest will then say aloud, 'You have declared your consent before the Church. May the Lord in His goodness strengthen your consent and fill you both with His blessings. That God has joined, men must not divide. Amen.

Church Of England Wedding Vow
from The Book of Common Prayer

Groom: I,_____, take thee,_____, to my wedded Wife, to have and to hold from this day forward, for better for worse, for richer for poorer, in sickness and in health, to love and to cherish, till death us do part, according to God's holy ordinance; and thereto I plight thee my troth.

Bride: I,_____, take thee,_____, to my wedded Husband, to have and to hold from this day forward, for better for worse, for richer for poorer, in sickness and in health, to love, cherish and to obey, till death us do part, according to God's holy ordinance; and thereto I give thee my troth.

Then, as the groom places the ring on the bride's finger, he says the following: With this Ring I thee wed: In the name of the Father, and of the Son, and of the Holy Ghost. Amen.

SHALEM SHABAZI

A Hebrew Wedding Song

translated by T. Carmi

My heart is bound to Hadassah in
love, but my feet are sinking in the
depths of exile. When will He give me
leave to go up and make my home
within the extolled gates of Zion?
Morning and evening I call to mind
the Princess. My heart and my mind
reel with desire. With sweet song I
shall shake off the pain of separation,
and then, my dearest, I will loudly
rejoice.

Now, my holy flock, fathom this song
I have composed. The bridegroom and
The bride have been crowned in wed-
lock, and this is a day for joy for the
majestic one, the precious one, for she
and her Beloved now endow each other
with grace and love. O my Beloved,
invite us all together to Your table and
Your cup, summon the remnants of
Your treasured people. And I shall
sing happily over this cup of salvation.

I shall disclose my mystic secret to
those who question me.

The wise and pure of heart are assured
of a good name, for they firmly rule
their passions. Their desire to do good
prevails. They will go up to the Garden
of Eden and inherit everlasting life. All
the love in my soul surges to the good-
ness of God. Blessed is He who rewards
each and every workman! May peace
flow over my flock like a river, over old
and young, over all the little children.

The Giving of Rings

CHARLES NICHOLL

A Handfasting
from The Lodger: Shakespeare
On Silver Street

Gifts would often be exchanged in token of the betrothal – typically, as today, rings. In one case, the man having brought no ring, a witness 'stooped down and made a ring of rush, and would have given it them'. Sometimes the ring is specified - 'a seal ring of gold with a picture of a white dog upon it, with the ears tipped with silver'. Hoop rings are also mentioned, like the one Marie lost out of her purse, and the double-hooped 'gimmel' ring, symbolic of clasped hands, was popular. On a gold gimmel ring of *c.* 1600, now in the Museum of London, is engraved a handfasting motto:

> As handes doe shut
> So hart be knit

Almost as popular as rings was the spouses' exchange of a piece or coin of gold, broken in half between them. Many other betrothal gifts are itemised – a pair of gloves 'worth 2s 6d', a petticoat, a 'peece of crimson rybbyn knit in a square knott wch she called a trew lovers knott', a 'jewell called an aggat', a prayer book, 'a French crowne and a tothepiker [toothpick] of silver', and so on.

These reports of handfastings in Elizabethan and Jacobean London help us to gauge something of the scene at Silver Street.

It is a brief, well-worn ceremony, balanced between a certain *ad hoc* casualness and a touching formality. This is a folk-rooted society, at ease with ritual. Shakespeare is not exactly officiating – the ceremony is precisely private rather than official: a 'contract in a chamber'. Legally speaking, he is no more than a witness of an oral contract. But often in these accounts there is someone obviously in charge, a master (or occasionally mistress) of ceremonies, and the phrasing of Daniel Nicholas's statement – 'they were made sure by Mr Shakespeare' – clearly suggests this. His role might indeed be summed up as 'directorial'. It is a scene to be acted out. There are lines to be spoken, and gestures to be got right, and props to be handled. It is not necessary that anyone else was present - a single witness was sufficient – but doubtless her parents were there, and perhaps others such as the maid Joan Langford, and Belott's mother and stepfather, the Fludds (but not, it seems, Mary's uncle Noel, who said he did not want to know the 'manner' or 'effect' of Shakespeare's involvement). And so for a few moments the Mountjoys' shadowy parlour becomes a little theatre, and a hush falls as Stephen and Mary take hands and speak their vows.

JACOB POLLEY

Dor Beetle

Scavenger on slug flesh, shit-eater,
I wear you on my wedding finger,
your black wing-case set in a plain gold ring.

Little clock, watchman, night-singer:
your six legs tick on my skin.

At the end of love, start burrowing.

ROBIN ROBERTSON

Wedding the Locksmith's Daughter

The slow-grained slide to embed the blade
of the key is a sheathing,
a gliding on graphite, pushing inside
to find the ribs of the lock.

Sunk home, the true key slots into its matrix;
geared, tight-fitting, they turn
together, shooting the spring-lock,
throwing the bolt. Dactyls, iambics –

the clinch of words – the hidden couplings
in the cased machine. A chime of sound
on sound: the way the sung note snibs on meaning

and holds. The lines engage and marry now,
their bells are keeping time;
the church doors close and open underground.

SEAMUS HEANEY

Wedding Day

I am afraid.
Sound has stopped in the day
And the images reel over
And over. Why all those tears,

The wild grief on his face
Outside the taxi? The sap
Of mourning rises
In our waving guests.

You sing behind the tall cake
Like a deserted bride
Who persists, demented,
And goes through the ritual.

When I went to the gents
There was a skewered heart
And a legend of love. Let me
sleep on your breast to the airport.

BENNETT HELM

Love as Union
from Stanford Encyclopedia
of Philosophy

The union view claims that love consists in the formation of
(or the desire to form) some significant kind of union, a 'we.'
A central task for union theorists, therefore, is to cash out just
what such a 'we' comes to—whether it is literally a new entity
in the world somehow comprised of the lover and the beloved,
or whether it is merely metaphorical. Variants of this view per-
haps go back to Aristotle (cf. Sherman 1993) and can also be
found in Montaigne (1603/1877) and Hegel (1997); contempo-
rary proponents include Solomon (1981, 1988), Scruton (1986),
Nozick (1989), Fisher (1990), and Delaney (1996).

Scruton, writing in particular about romantic love, claims that
love exists 'just so soon as reciprocity becomes community: that
is, just so soon as all distinction between my interests and your
interests is overcome' (1986, p. 230). The idea is that the union
is a union of concern, so that when I act out of that concern
it is not for my sake alone or for your sake alone but for *our*
sake. Fisher (1990) holds a similar, but somewhat more moderate
view, claiming that love is a *partial* fusion of the lovers' cares,
concerns, emotional responses, and actions. What is striking
about both Scruton and Fisher is the claim that love requires
the *actual* union of the lovers' concerns, for it thus becomes clear
that they conceive of love not so much as an attitude we take
towards another but as a relationship: the distinction between

your interests and mine genuinely disappears only when we together come to have shared cares, concerns, etc., and my merely having a certain attitude towards you is not enough for love. This provides content to the notion of a 'we' as the (metaphorical?) subject of these shared cares and concerns, and as that for whose sake we act.

...Friedman (1998), taking her inspiration in part from Delaney (1996), argues that we should understand the sort of union at issue in love to be a kind of *federation* of selves:

> On the federation model, a third unified entity is constituted by the interaction of the lovers, one which involves the lovers acting in concert across a range of conditions and for a range of purposes. This concerted action, however, does not erase the existence of the two lovers as separable and separate agents with continuing possibilities for the exercise of their own respective agencies. [p. 165]

Given that on this view the lovers do not give up their individual identities, there is no principled reason why the union view cannot make sense of the lover's concern for her beloved for his sake. Moreover, Friedman argues, once we construe union as federation, we can see that autonomy is not a zero-sum game; rather, love can both directly enhance the autonomy of each and promote the growth of various skills, like realistic and critical self-evaluation, that foster autonomy.

MICHAEL LONGLEY

An Amish Rug

As if a one-roomed schoolhouse were all we knew
And our clothes were black, our underclothes black,
Marriage a horse and buggy going to church
And the children silhouettes in a snowy field,

I bring you this patchwork like a smallholding
Where I served as the hired boy behind the harrow,
Its threads the colour of cantaloupe and cherry
Securing hay bales, corn cobs, tobacco leaves.

You may hang it on the wall, a cathedral window,
Or lay it out on the floor beside our bed
So that whenever we undress for sleep or love
We shall step over it as over a flowerbed.

VITA SACKVILLE-WEST

from Portrait of a Marriage

26 July [1920]

It was just then, however, that I first met Harold. He arrived late at a small dinner-party before a play, very young and alive and charming, and the first remark I ever heard him make was, 'What fun', when he was asked by his hostess to act as host. Everything was fun to his energy, vitality, and buoyancy. I liked his irrepressible brown curls his laughing eyes, his charming smile, and his boyishness. But we didn't become particular friends. I think he looked on me as more of a child than I actually was, and as for myself I never thought about people, especially men, under a very personal aspect unless they made quite definitive friendly advances to me first; even then I think one wonders sometimes what people are driving at.

I was eighteen then and he was twenty-three.

HOMER

The End of the Wandering
from The Odyssey

translated by Rev. Alfred J. Church

To her Penelope made answer: 'It is hard for thee to know the purposes of the gods. Nevertheless, I will go to my son, that I may see the suitors dead, and the man that slew them.' So she went and sat in the twilight by the other wall, and Ulysses sat by a pillar, with eyes cast down, waiting till his wife should speak to him. But she was sore perplexed; for now she seemed to know him, and now she knew him not, for he had not suffered that the women should put new robes upon him. And Telemachus said: 'Mother, evil mother, sittest thou apart from my father, and speakest not to him? Surely thy heart is harder than a stone.'

But Ulysses said: 'Let be, Telemachus. Thy mother will know that which is true in good time. But now let us hide this slaughter for awhile, lest the friends of these men seek vengeance against us. Wherefore, let there be music and dancing in the hall, so that men shall say, "This is the wedding of the Queen, and there is joy in the palace," and know not of the truth.' So the minstrel played and the women danced. And meanwhile Ulysses went to the bath, and clothed himself in bright apparel, and came back to the hall, and Athene made him fair and young to see. Then he sat him down as before, over against his wife, and said: 'Surely, O lady, the gods have made thee harder of heart than all other women. Would another wife have kept away from her husband, coming back now after twenty years?'

And when she doubted yet, he spake again: 'Hear thou this, Penelope, and know that it is I indeed. I will tell thee of the fashion of my bed. There grew an olive in the inner court, with a stem of the bigness of a pillar. Round this did I build the chamber, and I roofed it over, and put doors upon it. Then I lopped off the boughs of the olive, and made it into the bedpost. Afterwards, beginning from this, I wrought the bedstead till I had finished it, inlaying the work with gold and silver and ivory. And within I fastened a band of ox-hide that had been dyed with purple. Whether the bedstead be now fast in its place, or whether some one hath moved it – and verily, it was no light thing to move – I know not. But this was its fashion of old.'

Then Penelope knew him, that he was her husband indeed, and ran to him, and threw her arms about him and kissed him, saying: 'Pardon me, my lord, if I was slow to know thee; for ever I feared that some one should deceive me, saying that he was my husband. But now I know this, that thou art he and not another.' And they wept over each other and kissed each other. So did Ulysses come back to his home after twenty years.

EAVAN BOLAND

The Black Lace Fan My Mother Gave Me

It was the first gift he ever gave her,
buying it for five francs in the Galeries
in pre-war Paris. It was stifling.
A starless drought made the nights stormy.

They stayed in the city for the summer.
They met in cafés. She was always early.
He was late. That evening he was later.
They wrapped the fan. He looked at his watch.

She looked down the Boulevard des Capucines.
She ordered more coffee. She stood up.
The streets were emptying. The heat was killing.
She thought the distance smelled of rain and lightning.

These are wild roses, appliquéd on silk by hand,
darkly picked, stitched boldly, quickly.
The rest is tortoiseshell and has the reticent,
clear patience of its element. It is

a worn-out underwater bullion and it keeps,
even now, an inference of its violation.
The lace is overcast as if the weather
it opened for and offset had entered it.

The past is an empty café terrace.
An airless dusk before thunder. A man running.
And no way now to know what happened then –
none at all – unless, of course, you improvise:

The blackbird on this first sultry morning,
in summer, finding buds, worms, fruit,
feels the heat. Suddenly she puts out her wing –
the whole, full, flirtatious span of it.

KATHARINE TYNAN

Any Woman

I am the pillars of the house;
The keystone of the arch am I.
Take me away, and roof and wall
Would fall to ruin utterly.

I am the fire upon the hearth,
I am the light of the good sun,
I am the heat that warms the earth,
Which else were colder than a stone.

At me the children warm their hands;
I am their light of love alive.
Without me cold the hearthstone stands,
Nor could the precious children thrive.

I am the twist that holds together
The children in its sacred ring,
Their knot of love, from whose close tether
No lost child goes a-wandering.

I am the house from floor to roof,
I deck the walls, the board I spread;
I spin the curtains, warp and woof,
And shake the down to be their bed.

I am their wall against all danger,
Their door against the wind and snow.
Thou Whom a woman laid in a manger,
Take me not till the children grow!

ALGERNON CHARLES SWINBURNE

A Match

If love were what the rose is,
    And I were like the leaf,
Our lives would grow together
In sad or singing weather,
Blown fields or flowerful closes,
    Green pasture or grey grief;
If love were what the rose is,
    And I were like the leaf.

If I were what the words are,
    And love were like the tune,
With double sound and single
Delight our lips would mingle,
With kisses glad as birds are
    That get sweet rain at noon;
If I were what the words are,
    And love were like the tune.

If you were life, my darling,
    And I your love were death,
We'd shine and snow together
Ere March made sweet the weather
With daffodil and starling
    And hours of fruitful breath;

If you were life, my darling,
        And I your love were death.

If you were thrall to sorrow,
        And I were page to joy,
We'd play for lives and seasons
With loving looks and treasons
And tears of night and morrow
        And laughs of maid and boy;
If you were thrall to sorrow,
        And I were page to joy.

If you were April's lady,
        And I were lord in May,
We'd throw with leaves for hours
And draw for days with flowers,
Till day like night were shady
        And night were bright like day;
If you were April's lady,
        And I were lord in May.

If you were queen of pleasure,
        And I were king of pain,
We'd hunt down love together,
Pluck out his flying-feather,
And teach his feet a measure,
        And find his mouth a rein;
If you were queen of pleasure,
        And I were king of pain.

KATE CLANCHY

A Married Man

The married man dreamt last night
of a house that someone'd left him:
the sort of house you have in dreams,

a thousand rooms, one corridor. He wandered
round alone, he told me, smiled
his quiet, inward smile. *And found*

*the secret garden, high walled, locked, odd
velvet green. There, a window looked
towards the ocean.* He flexed pale hands,

I had, he said, *the key.* His wife touched
Their girl asleep, a lush and heavy animal,
and watched him, knowing, satisfied.

H. W. FOWLER

from A Dictionary of
Modern English Usage, 1926

wed is a poetic or rhetorical synonym for *marry*, & the established past & p.p. is *wedded*; but it is noticeable that the need of brevity in newspaper headings is bringing into trivial use both the verb instead of *marry* (DUKE WEDS ACTRESS), & the short instead of the long p.p. (SUICIDE OF WED PAIR); see INCONGRUOUS VOCABULARY; here is a chance for sub-editors to do language a service if they will.

THOMAS HARDY

At a Hasty Wedding

If hours be years the twain are blest,
For now they solace swift desire
By bonds of every bond the best,
If hours be years. The twain are blest
Do eastern stars slope never west,
Nor pallid ashes follow fire:
If hours be years the twain are blest,
For now they solace swift desire.

EDITH WHARTON

from The Age of Innocence

The result, of course, was that the young girl who was the centre of this elaborate system of mystification remained the more inscrutable for her very frankness and assurance. She was frank, poor darling, because she had nothing to conceal, assured because she knew of nothing to be on her guard against; and with no better preparation than this, she was to be plunged overnight into what people evasively called 'the facts of life'.

The young man was sincerely but placidly in love. He delighted in the radiant good looks of his betrothed, in her health, her horsemanship, her grace and quickness at games, and the shy interest in books and ideas that she was beginning to develop under his guidance. (She had advanced far enough to join him in ridiculing *The Idylls of the King*, but not to feel the beauty of *Ulysses* and *The Lotus Eaters*.) She was straight-forward, loyal and brave; she had a sense of humour (chiefly proved by her laughing at *his* jokes); and he suspected, in the depths of her innocently-gazing soul, a glow of feeling that it would be a joy to waken. But when he had gone the brief round of her he returned discouraged by the thought that all this frankness and innocence were only an artificial product. Untrained human nature was not frank and innocent; it was full of the twists and defences of an instinctive guile. And he felt himself oppressed by this creation of factitious purity, so cunningly manufactured by a conspiracy of mothers and aunts and grandmothers and long-dead ancestresses, because it was supposed to be what he wanted, what he had a right to, in order that he might exercise his lordly pleasure in smashing it like an image made of snow.

There was a certain triteness in these reflections: they were those habitual to young men on the approach of their wedding day. But they were generally accompanied by a sense of compunction and self-abasement of which Newland Archer felt no trace. He could not deplore (as Thackeray's heroes so often exasperated him by doing) that he had not a blank page to offer his bride in exchange for the unblemished one she was to give to him. He could not get away from the fact that if he had been brought up as she had they would have been no more fit to find their way about than the Babes in the Wood; nor could he, for all his anxious cogitations, see any honest reason (any, that is, unconnected with his own momentary pleasure, and the passion of masculine vanity) why his bride should not have been allowed the same freedom of experience as himself.

LOUISA SARAH BEVINGTON

Love and Language

Love that is alone with love
    Makes solitudes of throngs;
Then why not songs of silences, –
    Sweet silences of songs?

Parts need words: the perfect whole
    Is silent as the dead;
When I offered you my soul
    Heard you what it *said*?

G. R. M. DEVEREUX

*Describing Modern Manners and Customs of Courtship
and Marriage, and giving Full Details regarding the
Wedding Ceremony and Arrangements*

from The Etiquette of
Engagement and Marriage

Young Lovers

'Love at twenty-two is a terribly intoxicating draft,' says a writer,
and the sight of young lovers is one that softens all but the most
cynical. We smile at their inconsequence; tremble, almost, at
their rapturous happiness; yawn, it may be, over their mutual
ecstasies, still we know they are passing through a phase, they
are lifted for the time being out of the commonplace, and we
make excuses.

But these blissful young people are apt to take too much for
granted. Because Doris worships Harry it does not follow that
her family are to be inflicted morning, noon, and night with his
presence or his praises. She has no right to imply that every
moment spent apart from him is wasted. She has no call to give
up her share of household duties or to forsake her own studies,
just to wander about restlessly counting the minutes till he shall
come, or to spend the intervals between his visits in dressing
for his next appearance. She should not look bored directly the
conversation turns away from him, or exalt her idol over those
who have loved and cared for her since infancy.

Young Men who Woo Maturity

There seems to be a tendency nowadays for the surplus years to be on the woman's side. This is, in most cases, a grievous mistake. The girls are often to blame for it. In the pride of their youth they snub the young admirers whom they do not think worth their notice. An older woman knows how to heal the wound thus inflicted, and with her experience, her greater tolerance, and her charms mellowed, but not yet faded by age, she can win passionate devotion from one of these singed butterflies. She welcomes him with a dash of maternal tenderness in her manner, she takes an interest in his doings and subtly flatters his vanity, while her own heart is glad that she still has the power to please.

Middle-aged Lovers

No one would wish that the couple to whom love has come when youth has passed should take their pleasure sadly, but one does look for a self-restraint and dignity that shall be compatible with maturity. The woman of forty-five can love perhaps more deeply than the girl of eighteen. She can experience the full joy of being beloved; but she only exposes herself to ridicule if she takes the public into her confidence. It is not only bad taste to see such a one gushing over her lover, aping the little ways of sweet seventeen and coquetting like a kitten, telling the curious world, in fact, how rejoiced she is to be no more 'an unappropriated blessing.'

Poor soul! It may be that she has put through weary years of heart loneliness, but surely she might have learnt to hold her joy as sacred as her sorrow. Let her smarten herself up, by all means. Her happiness will suit nice gowns and dainty lace. Let her choose warm colours and handsome fabrics, and shun white muslin and blue ribbons.

CHARLES DICKENS

CHAPTER XXVIII: *A Good-humoured Christmas Chapter, Containing An Account Of A Wedding, And Some Other Sports Beside: Which Although In Their Way, Even As Good Customs As Marriage Itself, Are Not Quite So Religiously Kept Up, In These Degenerate Times*

from The Pickwick Papers

'Ladies and gentlemen—no, I won't say ladies and gentlemen, I'll call you my friends, my dear friends, if the ladies will allow me to take so great a liberty'—

Here Mr Pickwick was interrupted by immense applause from the ladies, echoed by the gentlemen, during which the owner of the eyes was distinctly heard to state that she could kiss that dear Mr Pickwick. Whereupon Mr Winkle gallantly inquired if it couldn't be done by deputy: to which the young lady with the black eyes replied, 'Go away'—and accompanied the request with a look which said as plainly as a look could do, 'if you can.'

'My dear friends,' resumed Mr Pickwick, 'I am going to propose the health of the bride and bridegroom—God bless 'em (cheers and tears). My young friend, Trundle, I believe to be a very excellent and manly fellow; and his wife I know to be a very amiable and lovely girl, well qualified to transfer to another sphere of action the happiness which for twenty years she has diffused around her, in her father's house. (Here, the fat boy burst forth into stentorian blubberings, and was led forth by the coat collar, by Mr Weller.) I wish,' added Mr Pickwick, 'I wish I was young enough to be her sister's husband (cheers), but, failing that, I am happy to be old enough to be her father; for, being so, I shall not be suspected of any latent designs when I say, that I admire, esteem, and love them both (cheers and sobs). The bride's father, our good friend there, is a noble person, and I am proud to know him (great uproar). He is a kind, excellent, independent-spirited, fine-hearted, hospitable, liberal man (enthusiastic shouts from the poor relations, at all the adjectives; and especially at the two last). That his daughter may enjoy all the happiness, even he can desire; and that he may derive from the contemplation of her felicity all the gratification of heart and peace of mind which he so well deserves, is, I am persuaded, our united wish. So, let us drink their healths, and wish them prolonged life, and every blessing!'

G. K. CHESTERTON

The Wild Weddings
from Manalive

'A modern man,' said Dr Cyrus Pym, 'must, if he be thoughtful, approach the problem of marriage with some caution. Marriage is a stage – doubtless a suitable stage – in the long advance of mankind towards a goal which we cannot as yet conceive; which we are not, perhaps, as yet fitted even to desire. What, gentlemen, is the ethical position of marriage? Have we outlived it?'

'Outlived it?' broke out Moon. 'Why, nobody's ever survived it! Look at all the people married since Adam and Eve – and all as dead as mutton.'

'This is no doubt an inter-pellation joc'lar in its character,' said Dr Pym frigidly. 'I cannot tell what may be Mr Moon's matured and ethical view of marriage—'

'I can tell,' said Michael savagely, out of the gloom. 'Marriage is a duel to the death, which no man of honour should decline.'

P. G. WODEHOUSE

from Uneasy Money

In the days that followed their interrupted love-scene at Reigelheimer's Restaurant that night of Lord Dawlish's unfortunate encounter with the tray-bearing waiter, Dudley Pickering's behaviour had perplexed Claire Fenwick. She had taken it for granted that next day at the latest he would resume the offer of his hand, heart, and automobiles. But time passed and he made no move in that direction. Of limousine bodies, carburettors, spark-plugs, and inner tubes he spoke with freedom and eloquence, but the subject of love and marriage he avoided absolutely. His behaviour was inexplicable.

Claire was piqued. She was in the position of a hostess who has swept and garnished her house against the coming of a guest and waits in vain for that guest's arrival. She made up her mind what to do when Dudley Pickering proposed to her next time, and thereby, it seemed to her, had removed all difficulties in the way of that proposal. She little knew her Pickering!

Dudley Pickering was not a self-starter in the motordrome of love. He needed cranking. He was that most unpromising of matrimonial material, a shy man with a cautious disposition. If he overcame his shyness, caution applied the foot-brake. If he succeeded in forgetting caution, shyness shut off the gas. At Reigelheimer's some miracle had made him not only reckless but un-self-conscious. Possibly the Dream of Psyche had gone to his head. At any rate, he had been on the very verge of proposing to Claire when the interruption had occurred, and in bed that night, reviewing the affair, he had been appalled at the narrowness of his escape from taking a definite step. Except in the way of business, he was a man who hated definite steps. He never accepted even a dinner invitation without subsequent doubts and remorse. The consequence was that, in the days that followed the Reigelheimer episode, what Lord Wetherby would have called the lamp of love burned rather low in Mr Pickering, as if the acetylene were running out. He still admired Claire intensely and experienced disturbing emotions when he beheld her perfect tonneau and wonderful headlights; but he regarded her with a cautious fear. Although he sometimes dreamed sentimentally of marriage in the abstract, of actual marriage, of marriage with a flesh-and-blood individual, of marriage that involved clergymen and 'Voices that Breathe o'er Eden', and giggling bridesmaids and cake, Dudley Pickering was afraid with a terror that woke him sweating in the night. His shyness shrank from the ceremony, his caution jibbed at the mysteries of married life. So his attitude toward Claire, the only girl who had succeeded in bewitching him into the opening words of an actual proposal, was a little less cordial and affectionate than if she had been a rival automobile manufacturer.

EDGAR ALLAN POE

from *The Bells*

I

Hear the sledges with the bells,
Silver bells!
What a world of merriment their melody foretells!
How they tinkle, tinkle, tinkle,
In the icy air of night!
While the stars that oversprinkle
All the heavens, seem to twinkle
With a crystalline delight;
Keeping time, time, time,
In a sort of Runic rhyme,
To the tintinabulation that so musically wells
From the bells, bells, bells, bells,
Bells, bells, bells—
From the jingling and the tinkling of the bells.

II

Hear the mellow wedding bells,
Golden bells!
What a world of happiness their harmony foretells!
Through the balmy air of night
How they ring out their delight!
From the molten-golden notes,
And all in tune,

What a liquid ditty floats
To the turtle-dove that listens, while she gloats
On the moon!
Oh, from out the sounding cells,
What a gush of euphony voluminously wells!
How it swells!
How it dwells
On the Future! how it tells
Of the rapture that impels
To the swinging and the ringing
Of the bells, bells, bells,
Of the bells, bells, bells, bells,
Bells, bells, bells—
To the rhyming and the chiming of the bells!

ARNOLD BENNETT

Marriage
from Mental Efficiency and
Other Hints to Men and Women

Sabine and other summary methods of marrying being now abandoned by all nice people, there remain two broad general ways. The first is the English way. We let nature take her course. We give heed to the heart's cry. When, amid the hazards and accidents of the world, two souls 'find each other,' we rejoice. Our instinctive wish is that they shall marry, if the matter can anyhow be arranged. We frankly recognise the claim of romance in life, and we are prepared to make sacrifices to it. We see a young couple at the altar; they are in love. Good! They are poor. So much the worse! But nevertheless we feel that love will pull them through. The revolting French system of bargain and barter is the one thing that we can neither comprehend nor pardon in the customs of our great neighbours. We endeavour to be polite about that system; we simply cannot. It shocks our finest, tenderest feelings. It is so obviously contrary to nature.

The second is the French way, just alluded to as bargain and barter. Now, if there is one thing a Frenchman can neither comprehend nor pardon in the customs of a race so marvellously practical and sagacious as ourselves, it is the English marriage system. He endeavours to be polite about it, and he succeeds. But it shocks his finest, tenderest feelings. He admits that it is in accordance with nature; but he is apt to argue that the whole

progress of civilisation has been the result of an effort to get away from nature. 'What! Leave the most important relation into which a man can enter to the mercy of chance, when a mere gesture may arouse passion, or the colour of a corsage induce desire! No, you English, you who are so self-controlled, you are not going seriously to defend that! You talk of love as though it lasted for ever. You talk of sacrificing to love; but what you really sacrifice, or risk sacrificing, is the whole of the latter part of married existence for the sake of the first two or three years. Marriage is not one long honeymoon. We wish it were.

'When *you* agree to a marriage you fix your eyes on the honeymoon. When *we* agree to a marriage we try to see it as it will be five or ten years hence. We assert that, in the average instance, five years after the wedding it doesn't matter whether or not the parties were in love on the wedding-day. Hence we will not yield to the gusts of the moment. Your system is, moreover, if we may be permitted the observation, a premium on improvidence; it is, to some extent, the result of improvidence. You can marry your daughters without dowries, and the ability to do so tempts you to neglect your plain duty to your daughters, and you do not always resist the temptation. Do your marriages of "romance" turn out better than our marriages of prudence, of careful thought, of long foresight? We do not think they do.'

CHARLES DICKENS

Chapter 31: The Wedding from Dombey and Son

Night, like a giant, fills the church, from pavement to roof, and holds dominion through the silent hours. Pale dawn again comes peeping through the windows: and, giving place to day, sees night withdraw into the vaults, and follows it, and drives it out, and hides among the dead. The timid mice again cower close together, when the great door clashes, and Mr Sownds and Mrs Miff, treading the circle of their daily lives, unbroken as a marriage ring, come in. Again, the cocked hat and the mortified bonnet stand in the background at the marriage hour; and again this man taketh this woman, and this woman taketh this man, on the solemn terms:

'To have and to hold, from this day forward, for better for worse, for richer for poorer, in sickness and in health, to love and to cherish, until death do them part.'

The very words that Mr Carker rides into town repeating, with his mouth stretched to the utmost, as he picks his dainty way.

GEORGE ELIOT

Marriage Bells
from Adam Bede

It was an event much thought of in the village. All Mr Burge's men had a holiday, and all Mr Poyser's, and most of those who had a holiday appeared in their best clothes at the wedding. I think there was hardly an inhabitant of Hayslope specially mentioned in this history and still resident in the parish on this November morning who was not either in church to see Adam and Dinah married, or near the church door to greet them as they came forth. Mrs Irwine and her daughters were waiting at the churchyard gates in their carriage (for they had a carriage now) to shake hands with the bride and bridegroom and wish them well; and in the absence of Miss Lydia Donnithorne at Bath, Mrs Best, Mr Mills, and Mr Craig had felt it incumbent on them to represent 'the family' at the Chase on the occasion. The churchyard walk was quite lined with familiar faces, many of them faces that had first looked at Dinah when she preached on the Green. And no wonder they showed this eager interest on her marriage morning, for nothing like Dinah and the history which had brought her and Adam Bede together had been known at Hayslope within the memory of man.

Bessy Cranage, in her neatest cap and frock, was crying, though she did not exactly know why; for, as her cousin Wiry Ben, who stood near her, judiciously suggested, Dinah was not going away, and if Bessy was in low spirits, the best thing for her to do was to follow Dinah's example and marry an honest fellow who was ready to have her. Next to Bessy, just within the church door, there were the Poyser children, peeping round the corner of the pews to get a sight of the mysterious ceremony; Totty's face wearing an unusual air of anxiety at the idea of seeing cousin Dinah come back looking rather old, for in Totty's experience no married people were young.

I envy them all the sight they had when the marriage was fairly ended and Adam led Dinah out of church. She was not in black this morning, for her Aunt Poyser would by no means allow such a risk of incurring bad luck, and had herself made a present of the wedding dress, made all of grey, though in the usual Quaker form, for on this point Dinah could not give way. So the lily face looked out with sweet gravity from under a grey Quaker bonnet, neither smiling nor blushing, but with lips trembling a little under the weight of solemn feelings. Adam, as he pressed her arm to his side, walked with his old erectness and his head thrown rather backward as if to face all the world better. But it was not because he was particularly proud this morning, as is the wont of bridegrooms, for his happiness was of a kind that had little reference to men's opinion of it. There was a tinge of sadness in his deep joy; Dinah knew it, and did not feel aggrieved.

JEAN SPRACKLAND

Third Day of the Honeymoon

She gets up before he wakes,
finds her dress inside-out on the floor,
puts on plastic shoes and goes down to the sea.

Sex has emptied her, she's forgetting to eat.
Salt cold rinses her sleek and girlish again,
raises bumps on her hairtrigger skin.
She jumps the waves, pulling faces
because no one's watching her.

The water licks and smacks, and it happens
quick as the word yes: the wedding band's tugged
over the knuckles and off.
She pulls up a few bunches of water, but really
she knows it's gone, glinting like a trick
somewhere down there in the shift
and tangle of deep life.

Later he'll kiss the thin white place, say
Never mind, I'll buy you another.
For now, she's properly naked at last.

VICTOR HUGO

from Les Misérables

translated by Julie Rose

There was tumult, then silence. The bride and groom disappeared. A bit after midnight, the Gillenormand house turned into a temple.

We will stop there. On the threshold of wedding nights, an angel stands, smiling, a finger to its lips. The soul enters into contemplation before this sanctuary where the celebration of love takes place.

There must be glimmers above houses like this one. The joy they contain must escape through the stones of the walls as light and dimly streak the darkness. This sacred and fateful celebration is simply bound to send a celestial shimmer into infinity. Love is the sublime crucible in which a man and a woman melt together; the one being, the triple being, the final being, the human trinity, the result. This birth of two souls in one must move deep night. The lover is priest; the rapt virgin filled with fear. Something of this joy travels up to God. Wherever there is a real marriage, meaning where there is love, the ideal is involved. A nuptial bed creates a pocket of dawn light in the darkness. If it were given to our eye of flesh and blood to see the fearsome and lovely sights of the higher life, we would probably see the forms of the night, winged strangers, the blue bystanders of the invisible, bend down, a throng of dark heads, over the luminous house, satisfied, blessing, pointing out to each other, sweetly alarmed, the virgin bride, and wearing the reflection of human bliss on their divine faces. If at that supreme moment, the new-lyweds, dazed with sensual rapture and believing themselves alone, were to listen, they would hear in their room the muted sound of fluttering wings. Perfect happiness implies the solidarity of angels. This little dark nook is overhung by the whole heavens. When two mouths, sanctified by love, come together to create, that ineffable kiss is simply bound to set the mysterious stars shuddering throughout immensity.

This is the real bliss. There is no joy beyond these joys. Love is the sole ecstasy here. Everything else weeps.

To love or to have loved is enough. Don't ask for anything more. There is no other pearl to be found in the shadowy folds of life. To love is an achievement.

The Blessing of
the Marriage

◈

EDWARD THOMAS

Sowing

It was a perfect day
For sowing; just
As sweet and dry was the ground
As tobacco-dust.

I tasted deep the hour
Between the far
Owl's chuckling first soft cry
And the first star.

A long stretched hour it was;
Nothing undone
Remained; the early seeds
All safely sown.

And now, hark at the rain,
Windless and light,
Half a kiss, half a tear,
Saying good-night.

FRANCES LEVISTON

Dragonflies

Watching these dragonflies
couple in air, or watching them try,
the slender red wands
of their bodies tapped
end to end, then faltering wide
on the currents of what feels to me
a fairly calm day,

I think of delicate clumsinesses
lovers who have not yet mentioned
love aloud enact,
the shy hands they extend
then retract, the luscious fumbled chase
among small matters seeming massive
as rushes are to dragonflies,

and in the accidental
buzz of a dragonfly against bare skin,
how one touch fires
one off again on furious wings
driven towards love and love, in its lightness,
driven the opposite way,

so in fact they hardly meet
but hang in the hum of their own desires.
Still, who would ask

these dragonflies to land on a stone
and like two stones to consummate?
How can I demand love stop, and speak?

MAUD CHURTON BRABY

Some Practical Advice for Husbands and Wives
from Modern Marriage and How to Bear It

'One doesn't want a lot of fine sentiments in married life – they don't work.' —W. Somerset Maugham

The most valuable piece of advice it is possible to give a couple starting on the 'long and straight and dusty road' of matrimony is: 'Blessed are they who expect little.' The next best is 'Strive to realise your ideal, but accept defeat philosophically.' It is difficult to live happily with a person who has a very high ideal of us; somehow it creates in us an unholy longing to do our worst. Miranda often says to me: 'The reason Lysander and I are so perfectly happy is because we never mind showing our worst side to each other, we never feel we need pretend to be better than we are.' Mark this, Bride and Bridegroom; remember a pedestal is a very uncomfortable place to settle on, and don't assign this uncomfortable elevation to your life's partner. More marriages have been ruined by one expecting too much of the other than by any vice or failing.

On the other hand, at the risk of being tedious, I must repeat that the most essential thing in Marriage is respect. It is above love, above compatibility, above even the priceless sense of humour. Respect will hold the tottering edifice of matrimony together when passion is dead and even love has faded. Respect will make even the 'appalling intimacy' endurable, and will bring one through the most trying disagreements, with no bruise on the soul, whatever wounds there may be in the heart. Therefore, Bride and Bridegroom, cultivate respect between you at all costs and, men and women, never *never* marry anyone you don't really respect, however passionately you may love. I believe one can be fairly happy in marriage without love, once the ardours and madness of extreme youth have passed. Without respect one can never be anything but wretched.

MICHAEL DONAGHY

Machines

Dearest, note how these two are alike:
This harpsichord pavane by Purcell
And the racer's twelve-speed bike.

The machinery of grace is always simple.
This chrome trapezoid, one wheel connected
To another of concentric gears,
Which Ptolemy dreamt of and Schwinn perfected,
Is gone. The cyclist, not the cycle, steers.
And in the playing, Purcell's chords are played away.

So this talk, or touch if I were there,
Should work its effortless gadgetry of love,
Like Dante's heaven, and melt into the air.

If it doesn't, of course, I've fallen. So much is chance,
So much agility, desire, and feverish care,
As bicyclists and harpsichordists prove

Who only by moving can balance,
Only by balancing move.

STEVE ROUD

Valentine's Day: Love Divination from The English Year

Last but not least of valentine traditions, the day (or its eve) was considered one of the key dates in the year on which love-divination procedures could properly be carried out. Many of these divinations were well known, such as sowing the hemp seed, in which unmarried girls threw hemp seed over their shoulders at midnight in hopes of seeing the forms of their future lovers following them. The following, as published by James Orchard Halliwell in 1849, is less common, but it is typical of the style of the day:

On Valentine's day take two bay leaves, sprinkle them with rose water and place them on your pillow, in the evening. When you go to bed, put on a clean night-gown, turned inside out and, lying down, say softly:

Good Valentine be kind to me
In dreams let me my true love see.
Then go to sleep as soon as you can, in expectation of seeing your future husband in a dream.

EUSTACE E. WHITE

Husbands and Wives in Sport
from Women at Home, 1910

Sentimental reasons apart, community of tastes is nowadays the chief basis of most marriages. Nowhere is this more evident than in the realm of sport. A plucky bit of straight riding on the hunting field, a graceful golf swing, a clever stroke at tennis, a daring descent on skis, an enthusiasm for hockey, have often stirred a sense of approval and sympathy which has subsequently developed into an affair of the heart. And in the resulting marriage there is likely to be a truer companionship than in the case of the husband and wife whose only interests are those of the home.

How desirable it is for married couples to share each other's tastes in sport is best argued by an instance of the opposite.

Regard, for example, the poor golf widow! She is a late-Victorian creation. Mark her *lonely* lot! Her husband spends his days on the links and his nights discoursing about the game. Patiently she must suffer this dull, this perennial talk of drives, putts, bunkers! The language of a Blackfoot Indian is as intelligible to her as the technical phraseology of the links. A story runs that one such wife inviting a friend to her house, wrote: 'If you play golf, bring your caddies and your bunkers, or whatever you call them, with you, and my husband will drive you to a meet.'

But times have been changing. Ignorance of this kind is scarce in the land. So are 'golf widows'. The latter have not pined away. They have been transformed from golf widows into golf wives. Affecting in self-defence the game which had so enslaved their husbands they speedily realised its enslaving charms, finally to become still greater slaves than their husbands. Now there is harmony in the home. Conversation is mutually intelligible and interesting, while there is no trouble over holidays. Every time it is a unanimous, if unimaginative, 'plump' for golf.

ANNE ELLISON

An Essay on the Choice of a Husband

Addressed to my tutor

A man to suit me
Must be loving and kind
With a generous heart,
An intelligent mind;
Honest and sober –
No spendthrift, nor mean,
But moving in that sphere
Which I call between

His countenance cheerful,
Clever his trade;
Not a coward, nor little,
But tall, and well made.
His age twenty-three;
With dark eyes and hair;
Not effeminate, nor childish –
For that I can't bear.

He must look straight before him.
As though he could see –
For I'll not have a man
Who is squinting at me.
He too must know how

To read write, and spell;
And be civil to all,
Then he's sure to do well.

Not passionate, mind,
But forgiving and free;
With a heart undivided
And constant to me:
With regular features –
Not too large, or flat;
Though if he was pious,
I should not mind that.

If I get such a husband,
I shall be glad;
I must mind how I choose though –
Some men are so bad.
But this I can say,
Without feeling afraid,
If I see none to suit me,
I'll die an old maid.

I've told you my choice,
So now I'll be neuter;
What there is to correct
I have left to my tutor.

ISABELLA WHITNEY

from *A Sweet Nosegay*,

or Pleasant Poesy, containing a
Hundred and Ten Philosophicall Flowers

36

Those strokes which mates in mirth do give
   do seem to be but light
Although sometime they leave a sign
   seems grievous to the sight.

63

Each lover knoweth what he likes
   and what he doth desire,
But seld, or never, doth he know
   what thing he should require.

106

Two eyes, two ears, and but one tongue
   Dame Nature hath us framed
That we might see and hear much more
   than should with tongue be named.

MILDMAY FANE

A Happy Life

That which creates a happy life
Is substance left, not gained by strife,
A fertile and a thankful mould,
A chimney always free from cold;
Never to be the client, or
But seldom times the counsellor.
A mind content with what is fit,
Whose strength doth most consist in wit;
A body nothing prone to be
Sick; a prudent simplicity.
Such friends as one's own rank are;
Homely fare, not sought from far;
The table without art's help spread;
A night in wine not buriéd,
Yet drowning cares; a bed that's blest
With true joy, chastity, and rest;
Such short, sweet slumber as may give
Less time to die in't, more to live:
    Thine own estate whate'er commend,
    And wish not for, nor fear thine end.

COLETTE BRYCE

Wine

The corkscrew lifts its elegant arms
like the Pope greeting tourists
on his balcony. Tonight we drink

religiously, fill to a shivering inch
of the brink, carefully, almost
warily. Tonight I drink to you,

and you to me, but this time,
seriously; as if following, word
for word in the clink, a ceremony.

MARY ASTELL

from Some Reflections Upon Marriage

An ill Husband may deprive a Wife of the comfort and quiet of her Life; may give her occasion of exercising her Virtue, may try her Patience and Fortitude to the utmost, but that's all he can do: 'tis her self only can accomplish her Ruin. Had Madame *Mazarine's* Reserve been what it ought to be, Monsieur *Herard* needed not to have warded off so carefully, the nice Subject of the Lady's Honour, nor her Advocate have strain'd so hard for Colours to excuse such Actions as will hardly bear 'em; a Man indeed shews the best side of his Wit, tho' the worst of his Integrity, when he has an ill Cause to manage. Truth is bold and vehement; she depends upon her own strength, and so she be plac'd in a true Light, thinks it not necessary to use Artifice and Address as a Recommendation; but the prejudices of Men have made them necessary: their Imagination gets the better of their Understanding, and more judge according to Appearances, than search after the Truth of Things.

KATHARINE TYNAN

Blessings

God bless the little orchard brown
Where the sap stirs these quickening days.
Soon in a white and rosy gown
The trees will give great praise.

God knows I have it in my mind,
The white house with the golden eaves.
God knows since it is left behind
That something grieves and grieves.

God keep the small house in his care,
The garden bordered all in box,
Where primulas and wallflowers are
And crocuses in flocks.

God keep the little rooms that ope
One to another, swathed in green,
Where honeysuckle lifts her cup
With jessamine between.

God bless the quiet old grey head
That dreams beside the fire of me,
And makes home there for me indeed
Over the Irish Sea.

JOHN DONNE

The Good-Morrow

I wonder by my troth, what thou and I
Did, till we lov'd? were we not wean'd till then?
But suck'd on country pleasures, childishly?
Or snorted we in the Seven Sleepers' den?
'Twas so ; but this, all pleasures fancies be;
If ever any beauty I did see,
Which I desir'd, and got, 'twas but a dream of thee.

And now good-morrow to our waking souls,
Which watch not one another out of fear;
For love, all love of other sights controls,
And makes one little room an everywhere.
Let sea-discoverers to new worlds have gone;
Let maps to other, worlds on worlds have shown;
Let us possess one world ; each hath one, and is one.

My face in thine eye, thine in mine appears,
And true plain hearts do in the faces rest;
Where can we find two better hemispheres
Without sharp north, without declining west?
Whatever dies, was not mix'd equally;
If our two loves be one, or thou and I
Love so alike that none can slacken, none can die.

CHARLOTTE MEW

On the Road to the Sea

We passed each other, turned and stopped for half an hour,
                                             then went our way,
    I who make other women smile did not make you –
But no man can move mountains in a day.
    So this hard thing is yet to do.

But first I want your life: – before I die I want to see
    The world that lies behind the strangeness of your eyes,
There is nothing gay or green there for my gathering, it
                                             may be,
                Yet on brown fields there lies
A haunting purple bloom: is there not something in grey skies
                And in grey sea?
    I want what world there is behind your eyes,
    I want your life and you will not give it me.

Now, if I look, I see you walking down the years,
    Young, and through August fields – a face, a thought, a
                        swinging dreamperched on a stile –;
I would have liked (so vile we are!) to have taught you tears
                But most to have made you smile.

To-day is not enough or yesterday: God sees it all –
Your length on sunny lawns, the wakeful rainy nights –; tell
me –;
        (how vain to ask), but it is not a question – just a call –;

Show me then, only your notched inches climbing up the
                                                garden wall,
                I like you best when you are small.

                Is this a stupid thing to say
                Not having spent with you one day?
No matter; I shall never touch your hair
Or hear the little tick behind your breast,
                Still it is there,
                And as a flying bird
Brushes the branches where it may not rest
                I have brushed your hand and heard
The child in you: I like that best.

So small, so dark, so sweet; and were you also then too grave
                                                and wise?
    Always I think. Then put your far off little hand in mine; –
                                                Oh! let it rest;
I will not stare into the early world beyond the opening eyes,
    Or vex or scare what I love best.

        But I want your life before mine bleeds away –
            Here – not in heavenly hereafters – soon, –
            I want your smile this very afternoon,
        (The last of all my vices, pleasant people used to say,
            I wanted and I sometimes got – the Moon!)

        You know, at dusk, the last bird's cry,
        And round the house the flap of the bat's low flight,
            Trees that go black against the sky
        And then – how soon the night!

No shadow of you on any bright road again,
And at the darkening end of this – what voice? whose kiss? As
                                        if you'd say!
It is not I who have walked with you, it will not be I who
                                        take away
Peace, peace, my little handful of the gleaner's grain
From your reaped fields at the shut of day.

    Peace! Would you not rather die
  Reeling, – with all the cannons at your ear?
    So, at least, would I,
  And I may not be here
To-night, to-morrow morning or next year.
  Still I will let you keep your life a little while,
  See dear?
      I have made you smile.

CHRISTINA ROSSETTI

A Birthday

My heart is like a singing bird
    Whose nest is in a watered shoot;
My heart is like an apple tree
    Whose boughs are bent with thickset fruit;
My heart is like a rainbow shell
    That paddles in a halcyon sea;
My heart is gladder than all these
    Because my love is come to me.

Raise me a dais of silk and down;
    Hang it with vair and purple dyes;
Carve it in doves, and pomegranates,
    And peacocks with a hundred eyes;
Work it in gold and silver grapes,
    In leaves, and silver fleurs-de-lys;
Because the birthday of my life
    Is come, my love is come to me.

from Amoretti

XVII

The glorious portrait of that Angel's face,
Made to amaze weak men's confused skill:
And this world's worthless glory to embase,
What pen, what pencil, can express her fill?
For, though he colours could devise at will,
And eke his learned hand at pleasure guide,
Lest, trembling, it his workmanship should spill,
Yet many wondrous things there are beside:
The sweet eye-glances, that like arrows glide,
The charming smiles, that rob sense from the heart,
The lovely pleasance and the lofty pride,
Cannot expressed be by any art.
  A greater craftsman's hand thereto doth need,
  That can express the life of things indeed.

ALICE OSWALD

Wedding

From time to time our love is like a sail
and when the sail begins to alternate
from tack to tack, it's like a swallowtail
and when the swallow flies it's like a coat;
and if the coat is yours, it has a tear
like a wide mouth and when the mouth begins
to draw the wind, it's like a trumpeter
and when the trumpet blows, it blows like millions …
and this, my love, when millions come and go
beyond the need of us, is like a trick;
and when the trick begins, it's like a toe
tip-toeing on a rope, which is like luck;
and when the luck begins, it's like a wedding,
which is like love, which is like everything.

APHRA BEHN

Love's Witness

Slight unpremeditated Words are borne
   By every common Wind into the Air;
Carelessly utter'd, die as soon as born,
   And in one instant give both Hope and Fear:
Breathing all Contraries with the same Wind
According to the Caprice of the Mind.

But *Billetdoux* are constant Witnesses,
   Substantial Records to Eternity;
Just Evidences, who the Truth confess,
   On which the Lover safely may rely;
They're serious Thoughts, digested and resolv'd;
And last, when Words are into Clouds devolv'd.

JOHN DONNE

from *An Epithalamion,*

or Marriage Song on the Lady Elizabeth and
Count Palatine Being Married on St Valentine's Day

I.

Hail Bishop Valentine, whose day this is;
    All the air is thy diocese,
    And all the chirping choristers
And other birds are thy parishioners;
    Thou marriest every year
The lyric lark, and the grave whispering dove,
The sparrow that neglects his life for love,
The household bird with the red stomacher;
    Thou makest the blackbird speed as soon,
As doth the goldfinch, or the halcyon;
The husband cock looks out, and straight is sped,
And meets his wife, which brings her feather-bed.
This day more cheerfully than ever shine;
This day, which might enflame thyself, old Valentine.

II.

Till now, thou warmd'st with multiplying loves
    Two larks, two sparrows, or two doves;
    All that is nothing unto this;
For thou this day couplest two phoenixes;
    Thou makst a taper see

What the sun never saw, and what the ark
– Which was of fouls and beasts the cage and park –
Did not contain, one bed contains, through thee;
  Two phoenixes, whose joined breasts
Are unto one another mutual nests,
Where motion kindles such fires as shall give
Young phoenixes, and yet the old shall live;
Whose love and courage never shall decline,
But make the whole year through, thy day, O Valentine.

III.

Up then, fair phoenix bride, frustrate the sun;
  Thyself from thine affection
  Takest warmth enough, and from thine eye
All lesser birds will take their jollity.
  Up, up, fair bride, and call
Thy stars from out their several boxes, take
Thy rubies, pearls, and diamonds forth, and make
Thyself a constellation of them all;
  And by their blazing signify
That a great princess falls, but doth not die.
Be thou a new star, that to us portends
Ends of much wonder; and be thou those ends.
Since thou dost this day in new glory shine,
May all men date records from this day, Valentine.

VII.

Here lies a she sun, and a he moon there;
  She gives the best light to his sphere;
  Or each is both, and all, and so
They unto one another nothing owe;
  And yet they do, but are

So just and rich in that coin which they pay,
That neither would, nor needs forbear, nor stay;
Neither desires to be spared nor to spare.
        They quickly pay their debt, and then
Take no acquittances, but pay again;
They pay, they give, they lend, and so let fall
No such occasion to be liberal.
More truth, more courage in these two do shine,
Than all thy turtles have and sparrows, Valentine.

VIII.

And by this act these two phoenixes
        Nature again restorèd is;
        For since these two are two no more,
There's but one phoenix still, as was before.
        Rest now at last, and we –
As satyrs watch the sun's uprise – will stay
Waiting when your eyes opened let out day,
Only desired because your face we see.
        Others near you shall whispering speak,
And wagers lay, at which side day will break,
And win by observing, then, whose hand it is
That opens first a curtain, hers or his:
This will be tried to-morrow after nine,
Till which hour, we thy day enlarge, O Valentine.

NICHOLAS CULPEPER

from Culpeper's Complete Herbal

Motherwort (*Leonurus Cardiaca*)

Descrip.—This has a hard, square, brownish, rough, strong stalk, rising three or four feet high, spreading into many branches whereon grow leaves on each side, with long footstalks, two at every joint, somewhat broad and long, as if it were rough and coupled, with many great veins therein of a sad green colour, deeply dented about the edges and almost divided. From the middle of the branches up to the tops of them, which are long and small, grow the flowers round them in distances, in sharp pointed, hard rough husks, of a red or purple colour, after which come small, round, blackish seeds in great plenty. The root sends forth a number of long strings and small fibres, taking strong hold in the ground, of a dark yellowish or brownish colour.

Place.—It grows only in gardens with us in England.

Time.—It flowers in July or the beginning of August.

Government and Virtues.—Venus owns the herb, and it is under Leo. There is no better herb to take melancholy vapours from the heart, and to strengthen it. It may be kept in Syrup or conserve; it makes mothers joyful, and settles the womb, therefore is it called Motherwort. It is of use for the trembling of the heart, fainting and swooning. The powder, to the quantity of a spoonful, drank in wine, helps women in sore travail, as also for the suffocating or rising of the mother. It provokes urine and women's courses, cleanses the chest of cold phlegm, kills the worms in the belly. It is of use to digest and disperse them that settle in the veins, joints, and sinews of the body, and to help cramps and convulsions.

WILLIAM SHAKESPEARE

Act IV Scene II
from Love's Labour's Lost

BIRON:
  … A lover's eyes will gaze an eagle blind;
A lover's ear will hear the lowest sound,
When the suspicious head of theft is stopp'd:
Love's feeling is more soft and sensible
Than are the tender horns of cockl'd snails;
Love's tongue proves dainty Bacchus gross in taste:
For valour, is not Love a Hercules,
Still climbing trees in the Hesperides?
Subtle as Sphinx; as sweet and musical
As bright Apollo's lute, strung with his hair:
And when Love speaks, the voice of all the gods
Makes heaven drowsy with the harmony.
Never durst poet touch a pen to write
Until his ink were temper'd with Love's sighs;
O, then his lines would ravish savage ears
And plant in tyrants mild humility.
From women's eyes this doctrine I derive:
They sparkle still the right Promethean fire;
They are the books, the arts, the academes,
That show, contain and nourish all the world:
Else none at all in ought proves excellent.
Then fools you were these women to forswear,
Or keeping what is sworn, you will prove fools.

For wisdom's sake, a word that all men love,
Or for love's sake, a word that loves all men,
Or for men's sake, the authors of these women,
Or women's sake, by whom we men are men,
Let us once lose our oaths to find ourselves,
Or else we lose ourselves to keep our oaths.
It is religion to be thus forsworn,
For charity itself fulfills the law,
And who can sever love from charity?

The Recession

SIMON ARMITAGE

In Our Tenth Year

This book, this page, this harebell laid to rest
between these sheets, these leaves, if pressed still
   bleeds
a watercolour of the way we were.

Those years: the fuss of such and such a day,
that disagreement and its final word,
your inventory of names and dates and times,
my infantries of tall, dark, handsome lies.

A decade on, now we astound ourselves;
still two, still twinned but doubled now with love
and for a single night apart, alone,
how sure we are, each of the other half.

This harebell holds its own. Let's give it now
in air, with light, the chance to fade, to fold.
Here, take it from my hand. Now, let it go.

W. B. YEATS

When You Are Old

When you are old and grey and full of sleep,
And nodding by the fire, take down this book,
And slowly read, and dream of the soft look
Your eyes had once, and of their shadows deep;

How many loved your moments of glad grace,
And loved your beauty with love false or true,
But one man loved the pilgrim Soul in you,
And loved the sorrows of your changing face;

And bending down beside the glowing bars,
Murmur, a little sadly, how Love fled
And paced upon the mountains overhead
And hid his face amid a crowd of stars.

MOYA CANNON

Arctic Tern

Love has to take us unawares
for none of us would pay love's price if we knew it.
For who will pay to be destroyed?
The destruction is so certain,
so evident.

Much harder to chart,
less evident
is love's second life,
a tern's egg,
revealed and hidden
in a nest of stones
on a stony shore.

What seems a stone
is no stone.
This vulnerable pulse
which could be held in the palm of a hand
may survive
to voyage the world's warm and frozen oceans,
its tapered wings,
the beat of its small heart,
a span between arctic poles.

ALICE FULTON

My Second Marriage To My First Husband

We married for acceptance: to stall the nagging
married friends who wanted us
to do it there and then—
with them. In the downy wedlocked bed
we ask 'Is there life after
one-day honeymoons to Kissamee Springs?
Was I all right?' The answers, woefully,
are no and no. And yes,

we lollygagged down the aisle, vowed
to forsake dallying, shilly-shallying, and cleave
only onto one another, to forever romp
in the swampy rumpus
room of our eccentricities: that sanctum
sanctorum where I sport
bedsocks and never rise
till noon. What did we know?
Did you know my love for animals
has always been acute? Perhaps in time
I will become a shepherdess, a jockey.

At the reception every table was adorned
with toilet tissue cy-
cloned into swans. When I unravelled one

to find the charm, the management
was shocked. Dismembering swans!
No bride had ever ... And the prize, a little gizzard
of a ring, was disappointing. Oh Person,
was it worth it? Of course,
we fit at dinner parties. But as one part warbles
to be normal, another puts a spin on things.
I see you striving to frolic
in your steel-mesh tweeds as I model
chiffon voluptuaries the colour of exhaust.

In the wedding album we end or commence
our revels. There we are! doing the cha-cha-cha
to the boom-chick-chick band
in our dyed-to-match togs.
We're getting fat
on the eats, foaming
white crumbs, 'Honey' and 'Dear'
cumbersome as live doves
on our tongues.

Bring squeezeboxes, gardenias,
a hybrid of the two. Congratulate us,
chums. Smile and freeze: our dimples stiffen
to resolute framed stares. How adult
we look! Our eyes burn
stoplights in the Instamatic squares.

JOHN DONNE

The Anniversary

All kings, and all their favourites,
All glory of honours, beauties, wits,
The sun it self, which makes time, as they pass,
Is elder by a year now than it was
When thou and I first one another saw.
All other things to their destruction draw,
Only our love hath no decay;
This no to-morrow hath, nor yesterday;
Running it never runs from us away,
But truly keeps his first, last, everlasting day.

Two graves must hide thine and my corse;
If one might, death were no divorce.
Alas, as well as other princes, we
(Who prince enough in one another be)
Must leave at last in death these eyes and ears,
Oft fed with true oaths, and with sweet salt tears;
But souls where nothing dwells but love
(All other thoughts being inmates) then shall prove
This or a love increasèd there above,
When bodies to their graves, souls from their graves
    remove.

And then we shall be throughly blest;
But now no more than all the rest.
Here upon earth we're kings, and none but we

Can be such kings, nor of such subjects be.
Who is so safe as we? where none can do
Treason to us, except one of us two.
True and false fears let us refrain,
Let us love nobly, and live, and add again
Years and years unto years, till we attain
To write threescore ; this is the second of our reign.

LINDA CHASE

Kiss in the Dark

She has thickened around the middle
like a successful custard
on a wooden spoon.
Her face has grown square, strong.

Her legs are sturdy with veins
showing at the backs of her calves.
Firm, muscular thighs fold slightly
Over her knees when she stands.

Skin blemishes, of course,
and bloating around the eyelids.
Her breasts begin to swell
halfway down her chest.

She won't let her upper arms show
and wears sleeves even when it's hot.
A well chosen standing collar
detracts from her throat.

She loves you, nevertheless.
At arm's length, she ventures
a first caress in the dark.
Will you go on from there?

JOHN BURNSIDE

Anniversary

What I believe in, now,
is woodwork and sea-grass,
the blond light on country roads and occasional
glimpses of the smaller birds of prey;

or lying awake at night, with a lamp still lit
in one of the lower rooms, to feel the darkness
gather like a fleece
above the stairs,

as if the house would happily reveal
its ghosts: umbrellas dripping in the hall
and rain tracked in from forty years ago
to other mirrors, other kitchen chairs.

Old conversations echo in our hands
and voices, all our lives
continuous and ready to be told
in words and gestures: unrecorded love

and what we take for love, on nights like this,
the cellar locked, the albums put away,
and some blind creature circling the roof,
its throat plucked clean, its feathers smudged with clay.

W. B. YEATS

The Collar-Bone of a Hare

Would I could cast a sail on the water
Where many a king has gone
And many a king's daughter,
And alight at the comely trees and the lawn,
The playing upon pipes and the dancing,
And learn that the best thing is
To change my loves while dancing
And pay but a kiss for a kiss.

I would find by the edge of that water
The collar-bone of a hare
Worn thin by the lapping of water,
And pierce it through with a gimlet and stare
At the old bitter world where they marry in
    churches,
And laugh over the untroubled water
At all who marry in churches,
Through the white thin bone of a hare.

FIONA SAMPSON

World Asleep

Darkness opens like a gate
again. My fingers on your latch
are tender when they lift the tongue,
slip a catch, then hesitate

across the entrance where you wait.
Your smile's a darkness joined to dark:
it widens as I close this gap –
almost noiseless. It's getting late:

nocturnal landscape – a country
I didn't choose – and I'm alone with you.
I kiss the soil. Its sweet reek
of straw's like longing, a snare of honey

to bite and bring me home to you:
a costly *heimat*. A world, asleep.

ANDREW MOTION

A Goodnight Kiss

When I come to the border around midnight
holding your amazingly light body in my arms,
your feet kick suddenly and we cross over.

There is your grandmother walking ahead of us
along a narrow ridge between the paddy fields
and *kiss-kiss* is the sound of her black sandals
making peace with the earth then taking leave of it.

LOUISE GLÜCK

Epithalamium

There were others; their bodies
were a preparation.
I have come to see it as that.

As a stream of cries.
So much pain in the world – the formless
grief of the body, whose language
is hunger –

And in the hall, the boxed roses:
what they mean

is chaos. Then begins
the terrible charity of marriage,
husband and wife
climbing the green hill into gold light
until there is no hill,
only a flat plain stopped by the sky.

Here is my hand, he said.
But that was long ago.
Here is my hand that will not harm you.

HUGO WILLIAMS

Love-Life

Her veil blows across my face
As we cling together in the porch.
Propped on the mantelpiece,
The photograph distils our ecstasy.
Each night we touch
The heart-shaped frame of our reliquary
And sigh for love.

Each morning we are young again –
Our cheeks brushed pink,
The highlights in our hair.
Our guests will be arriving soon.
We wait contentedly beyond the glass
For them to find us here,
Our smiles wrapped in lace.

DEREK WALCOTT

Love After Love

The time will come
when, with elation,
you will greet yourself arriving
at your own door, in your own mirror,
and each will smile at the other's welcome,

And say, sit here. Eat.
You will love again the stranger who was yourself.
Give wine. Give bread. Give back your heart
to itself, to the stranger who has loved you

all your life, whom you ignored
for another, who knows you by heart.
Take down the love letters from the bookshelf,

the photographs, the desperate notes,
peel your own image from the mirror.
Sit. Feast on your life.

The Sirens
from The Odyssey

translated by Rev. Alfred J. Church

'It was now evening when we came back to the island of Circe. Therefore we beached the ship, and lay down by the sea, and slept till the morning. And when it was morning we arose, and went to the palace of Circe, and fetched thence the body of our comrade Elpenor. We raised the funeral pile where the farthest headland runs out into the sea, and burned the dead man and his arms; then we raised a mound over his bones, and put a pillar on the top of the mound, and on the top of the pillar his oar.

'But Circe knew of our coming, and of what we had done, and she came and stood in our midst, her handmaids coming with her, and bearing flesh and bread and wine in plenty. Then she spake, saying: "Overbold are ye, who have gone down twice into the house of death which most men see but once. Come now, eat and drink this day; to-morrow shall ye sail again over the sea, and I will tell you the way, and declare all that shall happen, that ye may suffer no hindrance as ye go."

'So all that day we ate and feasted. And when the darkness came over the land, my comrades lay them down by the ship and slept. But Circe took me by the hand, and led me apart from my company, and inquired of what I had seen and done. And when I had told her all my tale, she spake, saying: "Hearken now to what I shall tell thee. First of all thou shalt come to the Sirens, who bewitch all men with their singing. For whoever cometh nigh to them, and listeneth to their song, he seeth not wife or children any more; for the Sirens enchant him, and draw him to where they sit, with a great heap of dead men's bones about them. Speed thy ship past them, and first fill the ears of thy comrades with wax, lest any should hear the song; but if thou art minded thyself to hear the song, let them bind thee fast to the mast.

'"So shalt thou hear the song, and take no harm. And if thou shalt entreat thy comrades to loose thee, they must bind the bonds all the faster."'

THOMAS HARDY
The Ivy-Wife

I longed to love a full-boughed beech
    And be as high as he:
I stretched an arm within his reach,
    And signalled unity.
But with his drip he forced a breach,
    And tried to poison me.

I gave the grasp of partnership
    To one of other race –
A plane: he barked him strip by strip
    From upper bough to base;
And me therewith; for gone my grip,
    My arms could not enlace.

In new affection next I strove
    To coll an ash I saw,
And he in trust received my love;
    Till with my soft green claw
I cramped and bound him as I wove ...
    Such was my love: ha-ha!

By this I gained his strength and height
    Without his rivalry.
But in my triumph I lost sight

Of afterhaps. Soon he,
Being bark-bound, flagged, snapped, fell outright,
And in his fall felled me!

CHARLOTTE MEW

The Farmer's Bride

Three Summers since I chose a maid –
Too young maybe – but more's to do
At harvest-time than bide and woo.
    When us was wed she turned afraid
Of love and me and all things human;
Like the shut of a winter's day.
Her smile went out, and 'twasn't a woman –
    More like a little frightened fay.
        One night, in the Fall, she runned away.

'Out 'mong the sheep, her be,' they said,
'Should properly have been abed;
But sure enough she wasn't there
Lying awake with her wide brown stare.
So over seven-acre field and up-along across the down
    We chased her, flying like a hare
    Before our lanterns. To Church-Town
        All in a shiver and a scare
    We caught her, fetched her home at last,
        And turned the key upon her, fast.

She does the work about the house
As well as most, but like a mouse.
    Happy enough to chat and play
    With birds and rabbits and such as they,
    So long as men-folk stay away.

'Not near, not near!' her eyes beseech
When one of us comes within reach.
    The women say that beasts in stall
    Look round like children at her call.
    I've hardly heard her speak at all.

Shy as a leveret, swift as he,
Straight and slight as a young larch tree,
Sweet as the first wild violets, she,
To her wild self. But what to me?

The short days shorten, and the oaks are brown,
    The blue smoke rises to the low grey sky,
One leaf in the still air falls slowly down,
    A magpie's spotted feathers lie
On the black earth spread white with rime,
The berries redden up to Christmas-time.
    What's Christmas-time without there be
    Some other in the house than we!

    She sleeps up in the attic there
    Alone, poor maid. 'Tis but a stair
Betwixt us. Oh, my God! the down,
The soft young down of her; the brown,
The brown of her – her eyes, her hair, her hair!

GUSTAVE FLAUBERT

from Madame Bovary

translated by Eleanor Marx

A gamekeeper, cured by the doctor of inflammation of the lungs, had given madame a little Italian greyhound; she took her out walking, for she went out sometimes in order to be alone for a moment, and not to see before her eyes the eternal garden and the dusty road. She went as far as the beeches of Banneville, near the deserted pavilion which forms an angle of the wall on the side of the country. Amidst the vegetation of the ditch there are long reeds with leaves that cut you.

She began by looking round her to see if nothing had changed since last she had been there. She found again in the same places the foxgloves and wallflowers, the beds of nettles growing round the big stones, and the patches of lichen along the three windows, whose shutters, always closed, were rotting away on their rusty iron bars. Her thoughts, aimless at first, wandered at random, like her greyhound, who ran round and round in the fields, yelping after the yellow butterflies, chasing the shrew-mice, or nibbling the poppies on the edge of a corn-field.

Then gradually her ideas took definite shape, and, sitting on the grass that she dug up with little prods of her sunshade, Emma repeated to herself, 'Good heavens! Why did I marry?'

She asked herself if by some other chance combination it would have not been possible to meet another man; and she tried to imagine what would have been these unrealised events, this different life, this unknown husband. All, surely, could not be like this one. He might have been handsome, witty, distinguished, attractive, such as, no doubt, her old companions of the convent had married. What were they doing now? In town, with the noise of the streets, the buzz of the theatres and the lights of the ballroom, they were living lives where the heart expands, the senses bourgeon out. But she – her life was cold as a garret whose dormer window looks on the north, and ennui, the silent spider, was weaving its web in the darkness in every corner of her heart.

She recalled the prize days, when she mounted the platform to receive her little crowns, with her hair in long plaits. In her white frock and open prunella shoes she had a pretty way, and when she went back to her seat, the gentlemen bent over her to congratulate her; the courtyard was full of carriages; farewells were called to her through their windows; the music master with his violin case bowed in passing by. How far all of this! How far away! She called Djali, took her between her knees, and smoothed the long delicate head, saying, 'Come, kiss mistress; you have no troubles.'

Then noting the melancholy face of the graceful animal, who yawned slowly, she softened, and comparing her to herself, spoke to her aloud as to somebody in trouble whom one is consoling.

LADY GRIZEL BAILLIE

Werena My Heart Licht I Wad Dee

There was ance a may, and she lo'ed na men;
She biggit her bonnie bow'r doun i' yon glen;
But now she cries, Dool and a well-a-day!
Come doun the green gait and come here away!

When bonnie young Johnnie cam' owre the sea
He said he saw naething sae lovely as me;
He hecht me baith rings and monie braw things;
And werena my heart licht, I wad dee.

He had a wee tittie that lo'ed na me,
Because I was twice as bonnie as she;
She raised sic a pother 'twixt him and his mother,
That werena my heart licht, I wad dee.

The day it was set, and the bridal to be
The wife took a dwam and lay doun to dee;
She maned, and she graned, out o' dolour and pain,
Till he vowed that he ne'er wad see me again.

His kin was for ane o' a higher degree,
Said, what had he do wi' the likes o' me?
Albeit I was bonnie, I wasna for Johnnie:
And werena my heart licht, I wad dee.

They said I had neither cow nor calf,
Nor dribbles o' drink rins through the draff,
Nor pickles o'meal rins through the mill-e'e;
An werena my heart licht, I wad dee.

His tittie she was baith wily and slee,
She spied me as I cam' owre the lea,
And then she ran in and made a loud din;
Believe your ain een an ye trow na me.

His bannet stood aye fu' round on his brow
His auld ane looked aye as weel as some's new;
But now he lets 't wear ony gate it will hing,
And casts himsel' dowie upon the corn-bing.

And now he gaes daund'ring about the dykes
A a' he dow do is to hund the tykes;
The love-lang nicht he ne'er steeks his e'e;
And werena my heart licht I wad dee.

Were I but young for thee, as I ha'e been
We should ha'e been gallopin' doun in yon green,
And linkin' it on the lily-white lea;
And wow, gin I were but young for thee.

SIR THOMAS WYATT

Whoso List to Hunt

Whoso list to hunt, I know where is an hind,
But as for me, *hélas*, I may no more.
The vain travail hath wearied me so sore,
I am of them that farthest cometh behind.
Yet may I by no means my wearied mind
Draw from the deer, but as she fleeth afore
Fainting I follow. I leave off therefore,
Sithens in a net I seek to hold the wind.
Who list her hunt, I put him out of doubt,
As well as I may spend his time in vain.
And graven with diamonds in letters plain
There is written, her fair neck round about:
'*Noli me tangere*, for Caesar's I am,
And wild for to hold, though I seem tame.'

WILLIAM SHAKESPEARE

Sonnet XVII

Who will believe my verse in time to come,
If it were fill'd with your most high deserts?
Though yet, heaven knows, it is but as a tomb
Which hides your life and shows not half your parts.
If I could write the beauty of your eyes
And in fresh numbers number all your graces,
The age to come would say 'This poet lies:
Such heavenly touches ne'er touch'd earthly faces.'
So should my papers, yellow'd with their age,
Be scorn'd like old men of less truth than tongue,
And your true rights be term'd a poet's rage
And stretched metre of an antique song:
    But were some child of yours alive that time,
    You should live twice; in it and in my rhyme.

SAMUEL DANIEL

Sonnet 39

When winter snows upon thy sable hairs,
    And frost of age hath nipt thy beauties near;
When dark shall seem thy day that never clears,
    And all lies withered that was held so dear:
Then take this picture which I here present thee,
    Limned with a pencil that's not all unworthy:
Here see the gifts that God and Nature lent thee;
    Here read thyself, and what I suffer'd for thee.
This may remain thy lasting monument,
    Which happily posterity may cherish;
These colours with thy fading are not spent,
    These may remain, when thou and I shall perish.
If they remain, then thou shalt live thereby:
They will remain, and so thou canst not die.

DOUGLAS DUNN

Land Love

We stood here in the coupledom of us.
I showed her this – a pool with leaping trout,
Split-second saints drawn in a rippled nimbus.

We heard the night-boys in the fir trees shout.
Dusk was an insect-hovered dark water,
The calling of lost children, stars coming out.

With all the feelings of a widower
Who does not live there now, I dream my place.
I go by the soft paths, alone with her.

Dusk is a listening, a whispered grace
Voiced on a bank, a time that is all ears
For the snapped twig, the strange wind on your face.

She waits at the door of the hemisphere
In her harvest dress, in the remote
Local August that is everywhere and here.

What rustles in the leaves, if it is not
What I asked for, an opening of doors
To a half-heard religious anecdote?

Monogamous swans on the darkened mirrors
Picture the private grace of man and wife
In its white poise, its sleepy portraitures.

Night is its Dog Star, its eyelet of grief
A high, lit echo of the starry sheaves.
A puff of hedge-dust loosens in the leaves.
Such love that lingers on the fields of life!

SAPPHO

Two Fragments

That impossible predator,
Eros the Limb-Loosener,
Bitter-sweetly and afresh
Savages my flesh.

Like a gale smiting an oak
On mountainous terrain,
Eros, with a stroke,
Shattered my brain.

Acknowledgements

I would like to express my sincere thanks to Laura Hassan at Vintage Classics for her support for, and tireless work on, the book.

SIMON ARMITAGE: 'In Our Tenth Year' from *Kid* (Faber and Faber, 1992), reprinted by permission of the publisher.

PAUL BATCHELOR: 'Pygmalion's Prayer to Venus' from *The Sinking Road* (Bloodaxe Books, 2008), reprinted by permission of the publisher.

COLETTE BRYCE: 'Wine' from the work *The Heel of Bernadette* (Picador, 2000), copyright © Colette Bryce, 2000.

EAVAN BOLAND: 'The Black Lace Fan My Mother Gave Me' from *Object Lessons* (Carcanet Press, 2006), reprinted by permission of Carcanet Press Ltd.

JOHN BURNSIDE: 'Anniversary' from *The Good Neighbour* (Jonathan Cape, 2005), reprinted by permission of The Random House Group Ltd.

MOYA CANNON: 'Arctic Tern' from *Carrying the Songs* (Carcanet Press, 2007), reprinted by permission of Carcanet Press Ltd.

LINDA CHASE: 'Kiss in the Dark' from *The Wedding Spy* (Carcanet Press, 2001), reprinted by permission of Carcanet Press Ltd.

KATE CLANCHY: 'A Married Man' from the work *Slattern* (Picador, 2001), copyright © Kate Clanchy, 2001.

FRANCES CORNFORD: 'The Avenue' from *Selected Poems* (Enitharmon Press, 1996), reprinted by permission of the publisher.

Index of Authors

Index of Titles and First Lines